Super Stitches
Knitting

Super Stitches
Knitting

ESSENTIAL TECHNIQUES PLUS A DICTIONARY
OF MORE THAN 300 STITCH PATTERNS

KAREN HEMINGWAY

Watson-Guptill Publications / New York

Contents

6   How to use this book

9   Knitting basics
10   Needles and other tools
12   Yarns
15   Instructions and charts
17   List of abbreviations
18   Holding the yarn and needles
19   Casting on
21   Binding off
22   Knitting
23   Purling
24   Increasing stitches
26   Decreasing stitches
27   Creating texture
30   Working with color
33   Making selvages
34   Correcting mistakes
36   Finishing
40   Caring for knitwear

43   Stitch library
44   Knit and purl patterns
62   Knit and purl panels
76   Ribs
90   Textured stitches
110   Edgings
130   Ornamental stitches
144   Eyelet patterns
162   Cables
186   Knitted lace
210   Textured colorwork
228   Fair Isle

249   Glossary
252   Index

HOW TO USE THIS BOOK

Knitting is one of those simple pleasures in life —it's easy to learn, relaxing to do, and is so convenient to pick up at any time. And you can produce gorgeous results with only a couple of stitches and a pair of needles. If you enjoy more of a challenge, there are thousands of stitches to explore, developed by creative fingers and passed on by generations of knitters. The most well-known, and many others, are gathered together in this collection for you to use in your own knitting and to share with friends.

Getting started
The book is divided into 12 main chapters. "Knitting basics" deals with all the know-how you need to start knitting. Beginning with the yarns and equipment, it moves on from how to control the yarn, to knitting and purling, to working with color, correcting mistakes, and finishing your knitted fabric.

The abbreviations in knitting instructions might be confusing when you begin to knit, but they will quickly become second nature. Any special abbreviations you need for a particular stitch are given in the written instructions, and the commonly used ones are listed on page 17.

Discovering stitches
Each of the other chapters is dedicated to a stitch family, loosely based on technique. On each spread, written instructions and/or charts appear on the left page, with a photograph of the knitted sample(s) on the right, so that you can see how the instructions relate to the finished piece.

"Knit and purl patterns" are just that—easy patterns made with simple knits and purls. Using the same stitches but in panels, the next chapter draws on patterns that often feature in the traditional British seamen's ganseys. Basic, functional ribs head the lineup in the "Ribs" chapter, which also presents a surprising variety of attractive alternatives. "Textured

stitches" will develop your skills by introducing twists, crossed stitches, and other techniques to create distinctive textures. "Edgings" offers a choice of neat hems, delicate lace, and flamboyant frills.

The last five chapters give you more chances to exercise your skills. If you're addicted to texture, try the bobbles and clusters, smocking and loops in "Ornamental stitches". "Eyelet patterns" introduces simple but charming lacy ideas. Next there is a wealth of cables to choose from—to combine on an Aran pullover or simply jazz up plainer knitting. Delicate and intriguing lacy patterns follow. Color streams into the next chapter, which shows how the slip stitch cleverly combines colors to create fascinating effects. And finally, a beautiful collection of Fair Isle patterns will inspire you to blend subtle shades or cool colors to your heart's content.

Enjoying the book
You can use this book in a number of ways, depending on your level of expertise:
- to look up a particular stitch, go to the index, which will refer you to the relevant page
- to select a stitch for a particular project, flip through the relevant chapter until you find a stitch you like
- if you are just beginning to knit, start with "Knitting basics" and then follow the instructions for some of the simpler stitches, perhaps in "Knit and purl patterns"
- or, of course, you can simply pop the book in your pocket or knitting bag and browse through the stitches for inspiration or share them with other knitters.

Left-handed knitters
Knitting is a two-handed skill, and many left-handers find that they can knit very easily in the right-handed way. If you do experience problems, the helpful Web site listed on page 256 gives a reworking of common abbreviations especially for left-handed knitters.

Knitting basics

This section tells you about the tools you need and the gorgeous yarns you can choose for knitting. You can also learn about or remind yourself of all the basic techniques so that you can explore the stitches with ease and pleasure.

NEEDLES AND OTHER TOOLS

You need just two tools to knit with—a pair of knitting needles—so you can knit anytime, anywhere. Your collection will grow steadily as you do more knitting, and you will probably want to acquire a few special needles. With a few general sewing tools, you're ready to go.

STRAIGHT NEEDLES

These are available in a wide range of sizes, from 0 (2 mm) to 15 (10 mm) and larger, to suit all yarns. The size to suit a particular yarn is usually given on the label. Two lengths are widely available— 10 inches (25 cm) and 14 inches (36 cm). You can choose from needles made of metal, plastic, wood, or bamboo, depending on the feel you prefer.

If you are using a metric or UK pattern, you will see a different sizing system; the equivalents of the metric and UK sizes are listed below.

DOUBLE-POINTED NEEDLES

These needles come in sets of four, or five for thin needles, so that you can knit with one needle and divide the stitches equally among the others. This allows you to knit in the round—circular knitting, which means the right side is always facing you and there are no side seams to sew up. Double-pointed needles are essential for circular knitting on a small number of stitches.

CIRCULAR NEEDLES

Circular needles are also very useful for circular knitting. Two short needles are joined by flexible nylon cord and are available in lengths from 16 inches (40 cm) to 48 inches (122 cm). Each length requires a minimum number of stitches to avoid overly stretching the knitting. Some knitters prefer to cast on using straight needles and transfer the stitches before knitting the first row. Always make sure that the cast-on stitches are not twisted before knitting the first row, as they cannot be untwisted later. Move a stitch marker up the rows before the first stitch on each round to keep track of where you are in the pattern.

CABLE NEEDLES

These short, double-pointed needles come in a range of sizes and help to transfer cabled stitches without dropping them.

OTHER TOOLS

There are a few other handy, though not essential, tools for knitting. A stitch holder secures stitches that are not being worked, but a length of yarn or large safety pin does the same job. Simple plastic or pretty beaded stitch markers identify particular rows that need matching up later or the beginning of rounds in circular knitting. A knotted loop of contrasting yarn performs the same task. A row counter slips onto the needle to record rows as you knit them. Plastic bobbins hold small lengths of yarn, which is especially useful for intarsia, or you can make your own with thin cardboard.

You will also need some sewing tools: a small pair of scissors, rust-proof dressmaking or straight pins for blocking, a tape measure, a ruler for measuring gauge swatches, a crochet hook for picking up stitches, tapestry needles for sewing up seams, and a notepad and pencil for making notes.

NEEDLE SIZES

US	0	1	-	2	-	3	4	5	6	7	8	9	10	10½	-	-	11	13	15
METRIC mm	2	2.25	2.5	2.75	3	3.25	3.5	3.75	4	4.5	5	5.5	6	6.5	7	7.5	8	9	10
UK	14	13	-	12	11	10	-	9	8	7	6	5	4	3	2	1	0	00	000

YARNS

There is such a rich diversity of gorgeous yarns from stores and Web sites to tempt you that it's difficult to know which to choose. Luxurious natural fibers are hard to beat, but some amazing synthetics and practical mixtures have also put in a recent appearance. Whichever yarn you choose, it should be suitable for the purpose—whether that's decorative or durable, fine or chunky—to get the very best from your knitting.

NATURAL YARNS

Wool has been the knitter's natural choice for many generations. It gives warmth, protects against the elements, and wears well. Woolen yarn has elasticity, which makes it easier to knit stitches that need lots of manipulation and keeps a finished garment in good shape. Wool also takes dye very well, so the yarn is available in soft, muted shades and bright, zingy colors. Particularly soft yarns are made from lamb's wool, which comes from the first shearing, and fine merino wool, which comes from the fleece of merino sheep.

Other natural fibers also make beautiful yarns, and the more expensive ones are often blended with wool. Silky, soft alpaca, from llamas and alpacas, is available in neutral shades and a range of soft colors. The Angora goat has long, luxuriant hair that produces strong, durable mohair, which is fluffy and has a slight sheen. Some people find it rather scratchy, but kid mohair is softer. Angora yarn comes from Angora rabbits and has very long, soft, fluffy fibers. It can be slippery to knit with and should not be used for items for young children because it sheds its fibers. Luxurious cashmere, from cashmere goats, is fine and light, soft and warm. However, it is not durable, felts easily, and must be washed with great care to avoid shrinkage. Silk is harvested from silkworm cocoons and makes a very strong and durable yarn.

Plant fibers also produce good knitting yarns. Cotton is available in a very wide range of colors, thicknesses, and finishes. It doesn't have the elasticity of wool and takes longer to dry, but it is strong and moth resistant. Mercerized cotton is processed to give it extra luster and strength. The flax plant produces linen yarn, which is heavier than cotton and therefore usually available in finer weights. It has an uneven texture and is often mixed with cotton.

SYNTHETIC YARNS

Although the tactile qualities of synthetics, such as acrylic, polyester, and viscose, are not as appealing as natural fibers, they do produce some very exciting yarns and are often mixed with natural fibers. They are strong, durable, and moth resistant; they are easy to care for and dry quickly, although they can lose their shape easily. They are also light, making them economical to knit with.

YARN THICKNESS AND WEIGHT

The thickness of a yarn is often described in terms of its ply. A ply is a single spun thread, and these threads are twisted together to make yarns that vary from very fine to super bulky. Most 2-ply, 3-ply, 4-ply, and DK (double knitting) yarns are made to standard thicknesses, but in fact a ply can be of any thickness, so general rules cannot always be relied on. If you want to substitute one yarn for another, it's best to compare them by knitting gauge swatches.

Yarn is available in several different weights, or thicknesses. Cobweb weight, as well as standard lace weight, yarns are suitable for knitting lace; fingering and baby yarns are often used for finer baby wear; and sport is a fine-weight yarn that lends itself to many fashions. DK is a good light-weight yarn. Worsted is a versatile medium-weight yarn; and bulky, or chunky, weight yarns are appropriate for heavier, outdoor pieces.

Novelty yarns, such as nylon or cotton ribbon, or metallic yarns, may not be composed of

twisted spun threads, but manufacturers will usually recommend the size of needles and a suitable gauge on the yarn label.

If you want to substitute one yarn for another to knit a particular design, make sure that it is the same weight and check that it knits up to the same gauge as the original yarn. Otherwise the finished knitting will inevitably be the wrong size. Also, compare the lengths per ball or skein of each type of yarn so that you buy enough of the substitute.

MANUFACTURERS' RECOMMENDATIONS

Yarn is available in balls, hanks, and skeins, and on spools and cones in quantities of .7 oz. (20 g) up. The most common weight is 1.75 oz. (50 g), although .88 oz. (25 g) and 3.53 oz. (100 g) are often found. Most yarn is sold with plenty of information on how to use it and take care of it— usually on the yarn label.

The yarn label gives you a lot of useful information—the composition of the yarn and its ply, the quantity in terms of weight and sometimes the approximate length, the shade and dye lot numbers, the recommended needle size and gauge, and care instructions. A comparison of the lengths of different yarns is useful if you want to substitute one for another. Always buy enough yarn from the same dye lot to complete a project—the same shade can vary considerably, and this is not always noticeable until you start knitting.

PERFECT FOR THE PURPOSE

With so many wonderful choices available, it is all too easy to fall in love with a yarn and feel it's impossible to leave it behind on the shelf.

TIP Don't join yarn in the middle of a row. To avoid this, either rewind the whole ball to check for breaks before beginning to knit or unravel enough yarn for each row (about three or four times the width of the row, depending on the stitch pattern) before you start it.

However, it is kinder to your pocket to give some careful thought to whether a yarn is suitable for what you want to knit. Think about whether your project needs to be durable or purely decorative, whether you want to knit something plain and simple, or if you are itching to get absorbed in complicated patterns.

The more tightly twisted the yarn, the more durable it tends to be and the better it will show up textured patterns. Plain colors also show off stitch textures and color patterns to the best advantage. Loosely twisted yarns such as bouclé or uneven yarns such as linen work well with plainer knitting on items that will have less wear. Random- and space-dyed yarns are also better suited to plainer knitting where the colors can drift unhindered rather than clash around textured stitches.

INSTRUCTIONS AND CHARTS

There are written instructions for all the stitch patterns in this book, except some of the Fair Isle patterns, and photographs of knitted samples show you the finished effects. Most of the Fair Isle patterns, and some of the others, are given as charts. Once you have made your choice, always knit a gauge sample, or swatch, before using a stitch pattern for a particular project.

INSTRUCTIONS

The written instructions are all in the same basic format. First there is information on how many stitches are needed. Cast on a multiple of the number given, plus any extra ones indicated to balance the pattern. Any special abbreviations and their explanations are given next. The right and wrong sides are always indicated, unless the knitting is reversible. Follow the instructions row by row, taking particular note of any repeated sections indicated by parentheses "( )" or asterisks "*". You might find it useful to mark off the rows as you go until you are familiar with the pattern.

ABBREVIATIONS

Knitting instructions use a lot of abbreviations, but you will soon become familiar with the most common ones, which are listed on page 17. Any special abbreviations appear at the top of the relevant written instructions. Always read through the instructions before starting to knit so that you understand the abbreviations and how the stitch pattern works.

CHARTS

The charts are laid out as grids to represent the pattern instructions in a visual way. The grid squares contain symbols or shading, which indicate individual instructions and are explained in the accompanying key.

Fair Isle charts

These charts are easy to follow and clearly show the finished pattern. Each grid square represents one stitch, and the pattern is shown with shaded squares against a background of blank squares. This gives you the greatest freedom to create your own color scheme, choosing dark and light tones to retain contrast and bring out the pattern.

The pattern repeat is given under the chart and is also indicated by one, or sometimes two, orange lines where it does not coincide with the outer edges of the grid. Cast on a multiple of the number given, plus any extra stitches shown to balance the pattern.

Work the pattern by following the chart rows from the bottom to the top. Start at the outer edge of the grid and knit the first row from right to left, repeating the pattern as necessary. Finish the first row with any stitches given to balance the pattern. If you are working on two needles, purl the second row, following the chart in the same way but from left to right. Continue working stockinette stitch in this way. If you are knitting in the round, knit all the rounds from right to left, using a stitch marker to indicate the beginning of the round.

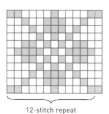

12-stitch repeat

KEY

□	background shade(s)
	pattern shade(s)
	start and end of the repeat

Cable charts

The instructions in these charts are represented by symbols, which occupy the appropriate number of squares for the number of stitches involved.

The rows are numbered up the sides of the chart—on the right-hand side for right side rows and on the left for wrong side rows.

Work the first row, starting at the appropriate outer edge of the grid. The first row will usually be worked from right to left, but some patterns start with a wrong side row. Start the second row from the opposite side of the chart and continue in this way, repeating the pattern until the panel is as long as required.

Knitted lace charts

These charts are also arranged to give a visual representation of the pattern, although each square and the symbol in it may represent an instruction involving more than one stitch. The number of stitches in some patterns varies from row to row, and where necessary this variation has been accounted for with shaded areas that are not part of the chart. The rows are numbered up the sides of the chart as they are for the cable charts.

Start each row at the outer edge of the grid and then work the repeat between the orange

lines as often as necessary for your total number of stitches. Finish the row by working any stitches on the grid after the repeat or to the end of the last repeat, shown by the broken grid line.

If you find working from a chart difficult, try using a row counter, marking off the rows, or underlining them with a removable self-sticking note as you knit. After one or two pattern repeats, you may find it easier to follow your knitting rather than the chart.

GAUGE

Gauge is the number of stitches and rows per inch of knitted fabric, based on the knitted stitch. Getting the gauge right is an important part of making a successful design. Always knit a sample, or swatch, at least 6 to 8 inches (15 to 20 cm) square to check that your gauge matches the measurements given in the pattern instructions—even a small difference can have a dramatic effect on the size of a garment.

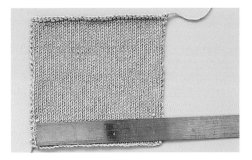

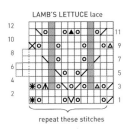

LAMB'S LETTUCE lace

repeat these stitches

KEY

	K on RS rows, P on WS rows
o	yfwd
/	K2tog
△	K3tog
\	SKP
▲	SK2P
V	inc K
✳	SK2P (SKP on last repeat)
⋏	sl2, K1, p2sso
✕	sl2, K1, p2sso, transfer to LHN, pass next sts over (sl2, K1, p2sso on last repeat)
	not part of the chart
	start and end of the repeat

When you have finished the gauge swatch, pin it on a flat surface. To check the stitch gauge, measure 4 inches (10 cm) along one row of the swatch and mark it with pins. Count the number of stitches between the pins. To check the row gauge, repeat the process vertically, counting the number of rows between the pins.

If your gauge does not match the pattern's, try working on smaller or larger needles. Making sure the stitch gauge is correct is your first priority—you can usually adjust the row gauge by knitting more or fewer rows than specified.

List of abbreviations

The most commonly used abbreviations are given in this table. Some stitches and patterns also require more specialized abbreviations; these are given, with explanations, above the appropriate written instructions.

alt	alternate
beg	begin(ning)
C2B	slip 1 stitch onto cable needle and hold at back of work, knit 1, knit 1 from cable needle
C2F	slip 1 stitch onto cable needle and hold at front of work, knit 1, knit 1 from cable needle
C3B	slip 1 stitch onto cable needle and hold at back of work, knit 2, knit 1 from cable needle
C3F	slip 2 stitches onto cable needle and hold at front of work, knit 1, knit 2 from cable needle
C4B	slip 2 stitches onto cable needle and hold at back of work, knit 2, knit 2 from cable needle
C4F	slip 2 stitches onto cable needle and hold at front of work, knit 2, knit 2 from cable needle
C6B	slip 3 stitches onto cable needle and hold at back of work, knit 3, knit 3 from cable needle
C6F	slip 3 stitches onto cable needle and hold at front of work, knit 3, knit 3 from cable needle
CN	cable needle
Cr2B	cross 2 stitches back (see page 27)
Cr3B	cross 3 stitches back (see page 27)
Cr2F	cross 2 stitches front (see page 27)
Cr3F	cross 3 stitches front (see page 28)
inc1 K	knit into the front and back of the next stitch to increase one
inc1 P	purl into the front and back of the next stitch to increase one
K	knit
K2tog	knit 2 stitches together
K3tog	knit 3 stitches together
kwise	knitwise
LHN	left-hand needle

M1	make one stitch by knitting into the back of the horizontal loop before the next stitch
P	purl
P2tog	purl 2 stitches together
P3tog	purl 3 stitches together
P4tog	purl 4 stitches together
pwise	purlwise
psso	pass slipped stitch over
p2sso	pass 2 slipped stitches over
rem	remain(ing)
rep	repeat
RHN	right-hand needle
RS	right side
SKP	slip 1 stitch, knit 1, pass slipped stitch over
SK2P	slip 1 stitch, knit 2 stitches together, pass slipped stitch over
SK3P	slip 1 stitch, knit 3 stitches together, pass slipped stitch over
SPP	slip 1 stitch, purl 1, pass slipped stitch over
SP2P	slip 1 stitch, purl 2 stitches together, pass slipped stitch over
sl1	slip 1 stitch purlwise (unless otherwise instructed)
sl1k	slip 1 stitch knitwise
sl2k	slip 2 stitches knitwise
st(s)	stitch(es)
St st	stockinette stitch
T2B	twist 2 stitches back (see page 27)
T2F	twist 2 stitches front (see page 27)
tbl	through back loop
tfl	through front loop
tog	together
WS	wrong side
ybk (or yb)	yarn to the back
ybrn	yarn to the back and round needle (knit next stitch)
yfrn	yarn forward and round needle (purl next stitch)
yfwd (or yf)	yarn forward, or to the front (knit next stitch)
yon	yarn over needle
yrn	yarn round needle (purl next stitch)

HOLDING THE YARN AND NEEDLES

There are two basic methods of holding the yarn, so practice until you find the one that is most comfortable. You could wrap the yarn around more or fewer fingers than described here as long as it flows freely and you maintain a consistent tension. If you can master both methods, you will be able to work a different colored yarn with each hand, which is very useful for stranding and weaving (see pages 30 and 31).

Hold a knitting needle in each hand, with one thumb lying along each needle and one index finger resting near each tip. Curl the rest of your fingers under to support the needles. The left-hand needle holds the stitches ready to be worked, and the new stitches are passed onto the right-hand needle.

HOLDING THE YARN IN THE RIGHT HAND
With the right palm facing up, take the end of the yarn from the ball and pass it between the little and ring fingers, around the back of the little finger, in front of the ring and middle fingers, and behind the index finger (1).

(1)

Use the right index finger to pass the yarn around the needle tip to make new stitches, while the loop around the little finger regulates the yarn tension. Control the existing stitches and tips of both needles with the left index finger and thumb.

HOLDING THE YARN IN THE LEFT HAND
With the left palm facing up, pass the yarn from the ball between the little and ring fingers, around the little finger, in front of the ring and middle fingers, and behind the index finger (2).

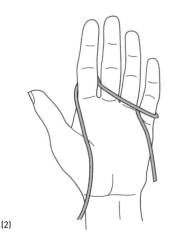

(2)

Control the yarn by holding it taut between the needle and the left index finger. Use the thumb to control the existing stitches and the needle tip. Control the new stitches with the right index finger and thumb, using the needle tip to pull the yarn through.

CASTING ON

Casting on gives you a number of stitches as a foundation for the rest of your knitting. Each method produces a slightly different edge, appropriate for different kinds of knitting. A slip knot makes the first stitch.

MAKING A SLIP KNOT

Make a loop in the yarn about 8 inches (20 cm) from the cut end. Holding both yarn ends in one hand, slip a knitting needle tip under the loop, and pull the needle upward to make the knot (1). Pull the yarn attached to the ball to tighten the knot around the needle or the cut end to loosen it.

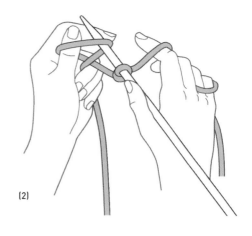

(2)

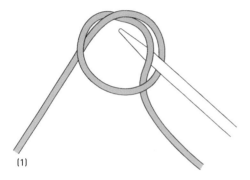

(1)

THUMB CAST-ON

Using one needle, this method is easy for beginners and produces a fairly elastic edge.

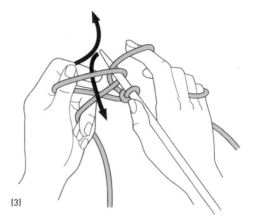

(3)

Make a slip knot some distance from the cut end of the yarn—calculate about 3/4 inch (2 cm) for every stitch you need to cast on. Slip the slip knot on the needle. Hold the needle and ball end of the yarn in the right hand, controlling the yarn with the right index finger. Hold the cut end of the yarn in the left hand and wrap it once around the left thumb, from front to back. Insert the needle tip under the loop around the thumb (2). Wind the ball end over the needle tip (3). Bring the loop on the thumb over the needle tip, remove the thumb, and gently pull on the cut end to tighten the stitch (4). Repeat the process until you have the required number of stitches.

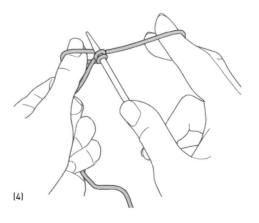

(4)

KNIT-ON CAST-ON

Using two needles, this versatile method produces a soft edge when worked through the loop fronts and a firm edge when worked through the backs.

Place a slip knot on the left-hand needle and insert the tip of the right-hand needle into the loop. Wind the ball end of the yarn around the tip of the right-hand needle (5).

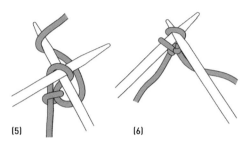

(5)　　　　　　　　　(6)

Slide the right-hand needle back, and with the tip pull the yarn through the slip knot to make a new stitch. Slip the new stitch onto the left-hand needle, making sure that it lies in the same direction (6). Without withdrawing the right-hand needle, repeat until you have the required number of stitches.

CABLE CAST-ON

This method, using two needles, produces a firm, durable edge.

Make the first two stitches as you did for the knit-on cast-on method, transferring the new stitch onto the left-hand needle and withdrawing the right-hand needle. Insert the right-hand needle between the two stitches. Make a new stitch and transfer it to the left-hand needle as

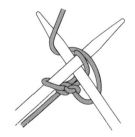

(7)

before (7). Repeat until you have the required number of stitches.

SINGLE CAST-ON

This method, using one needle, produces a delicate edge particularly suitable for lace.

Hold the needle with a slip knot on it in the right hand and the ball end of the yarn in the left hand. Wrap the yarn over and around the left thumb to make a loop. Bring the tip of the needle up through the loop to make a new stitch (8) and gently pull the yarn to tighten the stitch around the needle. Repeat until you have the required number of stitches.

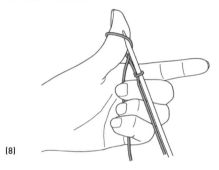

(8)

INVISIBLE CAST-ON

This two-needle method is ideal for producing a durable edge for single ribbing.

Cast on half the number of stitches required using the cable cast-on method (see left). Cast on an extra stitch if required to give an even number. Starting with a purl row, work two rows of stockinette stitch in a contrasting color and then four rows in the main yarn.

On the next row, purl one stitch. Using the right-hand needle, pick up the loop directly below on the first row of the main yarn. Transfer the loop to the left-hand needle and knit it. Repeat along the whole row until there is one fewer than twice the original number of stitches. Work the required number of rows for the ribbing. Draw the loose end of contrasting yarn up tight and cut it to release the first few edging stitches. Repeat until the contrasting yarn has been removed.

BINDING OFF

Binding off securely binds the last row of knitting or starts the shaping for an armhole or neckline.

BASIC BIND-OFF

This most frequently used method forms a firm, neat edge. Bind off in pattern on the right side, knitting the knit and purling the purl stitches unless directed otherwise. Make sure to keep the stitches even and relatively loose.

Work the first two stitches on the row in pattern. Hold the yarn to the back of the work and insert the tip of the left-hand needle into the front of the first stitch (on the right-hand needle) from left to right. Lift the first stitch over the second one and off the needle (1). This is counted as one bind-off stitch.

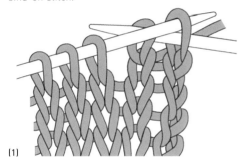

(1)

Work the next stitch and repeat the process until the required number of stitches have been bound off.

SEAM BIND-OFF

Use this method to form an almost invisible join between two edges with the same number of stitches. It is ideal for a shoulder seam on which none of the stitches have previously been bound off and a firm finish is not appropriate. You will need three knitting needles.

Hold the two pieces of knitting in the left hand with the right sides facing and the needle tips in the same direction. Insert the tip of the third needle through the back of the first stitch on the front needle and the front of the first stitch on the back needle (2).

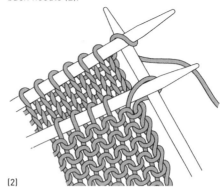

(2)

Knit the two stitches together. Then knit the second pair of stitches together in the same way. Using the tip of one of the left-hand needles, bring the first stitch on the right-hand needle over the second one and drop it off the needle. Continue binding off pairs of stitches in this way.

SECURING THE YARN END

When all the stitches are bound off, cut the yarn, leaving a long end for sewing up, and slip it through the last loop (3). Pull the yarn to tighten the loop.

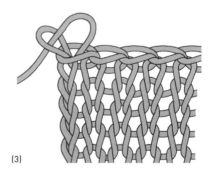

(3)

TIP If your knitting tends to be tight or you specifically want to bind off loosely, use a pair of needles one or two sizes bigger than those used for the main knitting.

KNITTING

The knit stitch is one of the two basic stitches in knitting. The yarn is held at the back of the work and forms a flat, vertical loop on the right side of the knitting. The two methods shown here give you a choice of controlling the working yarn with the right or the left hand, although the stitches are always knitted from the left-hand needle to form a new row of stitches on the right-hand needle.

RIGHT-HANDED METHOD

Hold the needle with the stitches in the left hand and the working yarn to the back of the work in the right hand (see page 18). Insert the tip of the right-hand needle into the front of the first stitch from left to right. Wrap the yarn around the tip of the right-hand needle from back to front (1). Pull the right-hand needle down, drawing the yarn through the stitch (2). Push the tip of the left-hand needle with the right index finger and slip the stitch off the left-hand needle onto the right one. Repeat until all the stitches have been knitted and transferred to form the new row.

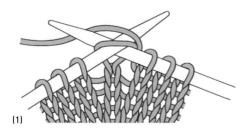

(1)

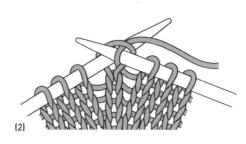

(2)

LEFT-HANDED METHOD

Hold the working yarn (see page 18) and also the needle with the stitches in the left hand. Holding the yarn to the back of the work, insert the tip of the right-hand needle into the front of the first stitch from left to right. Rotate the tip of the right-hand needle under and behind the yarn (3).

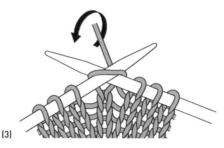

(3)

Pull the right-hand needle down, drawing the yarn through the stitch (4). Slip the stitch off onto the right-hand needle as for the right-handed method. Repeat to complete the new row.

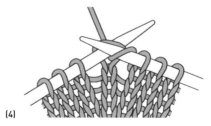

(4)

PURLING

The second basic stitch is the purl stitch, the reverse of the knit stitch. The yarn is held at the front of the work and forms a horizontal loop on the right side of the knitting. You can control the working yarn with the right or the left hand for this stitch too.

RIGHT-HANDED METHOD

Hold the needle with the stitches in the left hand and the working yarn to the front of the work in the right hand (see page 18). Insert the tip of the right-hand needle into the front of the first stitch from right to left. Wrap the yarn around the tip of the right-hand needle from front to back (1). Pull the right-hand needle down, drawing the yarn through the stitch (2). Push the tip of the left-hand needle with the right index finger and slip the stitch onto the right-hand needle. Repeat until all the stitches have been knitted and transferred to form the new row.

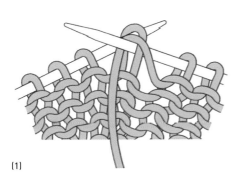

(1)

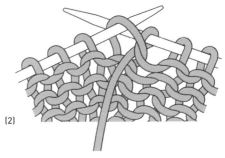

(2)

LEFT-HANDED METHOD

Hold the working yarn (see page 18) and the needle with the stitches in the left hand. Holding the yarn to the front of the work, insert the tip of the right-hand needle into the front of the first stitch from right to left (3). Rotate the left wrist so the working yarn comes toward you. Rotate the tip of the right-hand needle down over the yarn and back, and then draw the loop through the stitch (4). Slip the stitch onto the right-hand needle as for the right-handed method. Repeat to complete the new row.

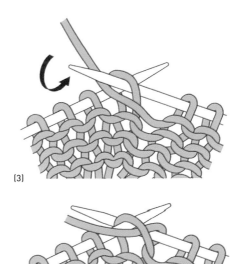

(3)

(4)

INCREASING STITCHES

There are various methods of increasing stitches either to make the whole piece of knitting wider or as a component in creating textured or lacy patterns.

BAR INCREASE (INCREASE A STITCH)

This method produces a tiny bar across the increased stitch, which makes it easy to count the increases. It is useful for increasing one stitch at the beginning or end of a row. The bar is formed after the worked stitch, so at the end of a row work the increase in the stitch before the last one.

Knitwise

◆ inc1 K (increase 1 knit stitch)

Knit into the front of the stitch as usual but do not slip the stitch off the left-hand needle. Knit into the same stitch again through the back of the loop (1) and then slip both stitches off the needle.

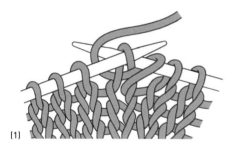

(1)

Purlwise

◆ inc1 P (increase 1 purl stitch)

Purl into the front of the stitch as usual but do not slip the stitch off the left-hand needle. Purl into the same stitch again through the back of the loop (2) and then slip both stitches off the needle.

> **TIP** To make more tailored shaping and keep a firm edge, make any increases or decreases a few stitches in from the edge.

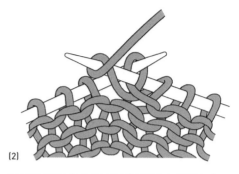

(2)

MAKE ONE INCREASE (MAKE A STITCH)

There are various ways of making one extra stitch. You can use the following method knitwise or purlwise, especially to make nearly invisible increases on the first row of a garment after the ribbing.

◆ M1 (make 1 stitch)

With the tip of the right-hand needle, lift the yarn between the stitch just worked and the next one and slip it onto the left-hand needle. Work a stitch into the back of the loop (3) and transfer it to the right-hand needle as usual.

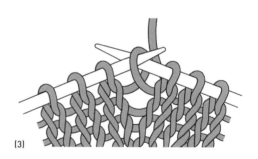

(3)

YARN-OVER INCREASE

◆ yon (yarn over needle)

This is a generic instruction for creating an extra stitch, and a tiny hole, usually in the middle of the row. It is particularly useful, followed by a decrease, in eyelet and lace patterns, and can be used to make small buttonholes. "yfwd" (or "yf") and "yrn" are the more specific abbreviations for the same effect.

◆ **yfwd/yf (yarn forward, or to the front)**
Use this method when the next stitch is a knit stitch. Start with the yarn at, or bring it to, the front of the work. Take the yarn over the right-hand needle to knit the next stitch in the usual way, forming an extra stitch as you do so (4).

the back (6) and then the front of the same stitch to make three stitches in total. If you want to make more than three, continue knitting into the back and front of the original stitch and slip it off the left-hand needle when you have enough new stitches.

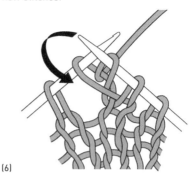

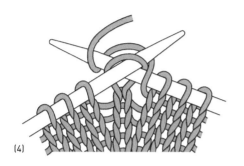

(4)

◆ **yrn (yarn round needle)**
Use this method when the next stitch is a purl stitch. Bring the yarn to the front of the work if it is not already there. Take the yarn over the right-hand needle and then under it, returning it to the front of the work, forming the extra stitch (5). Purl the next stitch.

(6)

Purlwise
Purl into the front, the back, and the front of the stitch again, but do not slip it off the left-hand needle. Continue to make more new stitches in the same way if you need them and then slip the original stitch off the left-hand needle.

CAST-ON STITCHES
Adding a number of stitches at the beginning of a row can be done simply by casting them on, starting from the first existing stitch. You can do this using the knit-on or thumb method (pages 20 and 19).

(5)

MULTIPLE INCREASE STITCHES
You may need to make three or more stitches from one stitch when creating textured effects such as bobbles.

> **TIP** Make a multiple yarn over—for example, wrap the yarn around the needle two or more times—to form a bigger hole. Form the extra stitches by knitting and purling into the yarn over on the following row.

Knitwise
Knit into the front of the existing stitch as usual, but do not slip it off the left-hand needle. Knit into

DECREASING STITCHES

There are various methods of decreasing stitches either to make the knitting narrower or as a component in textured or lacy patterns.

WORKING TWO STITCHES TOGETHER

◆ K2tog or P2tog (knit/purl 2 together)

This method makes the stitches slant to the right and is often used to decrease one stitch at the end of a row of stockinette stitch or in a lace or eyelet pattern. It can also be used to knit or purl three stitches together (K3tog or P3tog).

Insert the right-hand needle into the front of the next two stitches and knit (1) or purl them together as one stitch, according to the pattern.

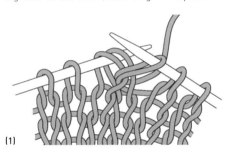

(1)

◆ K2tog tbl or P2tog tbl (knit/purl 2 together through back loops)

Here the stitches slant to the left. The same method can also be used to knit or purl three stitches together through the back loops (K3tog tbl or P3tog tbl).

Slip the next two stitches knitwise, one by one, onto the right-hand needle and then right back

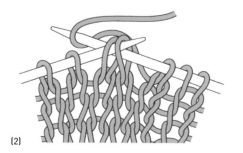

(2)

onto the left-hand needle, effectively untwisting them. Then knit (2) or purl (according to the instructions) the same two stitches through the back loops—now much easier to do.

SLIP STITCH DECREASE

◆ SKP (slip 1, knit 1, pass slip stitch over)

This method slants the decreased stitch to the left and is often used to decrease one stitch at the beginning of a row of stockinette stitch.

Slip the next stitch onto the right-hand needle. Knit the next stitch. Insert the left-hand needle into the front of the slipped stitch and pass it over the knitted stitch (3) and drop it off the needle.

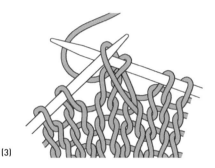

(3)

◆ SPP (slip 1, purl 1, pass slip stitch over)

Purl the first stitch, but return it to the left hand needle. Insert the right-hand needle into the front of the next stitch and pass it over the knitted stitch (4). Transfer that stitch to the right-hand needle.

You can also decrease two stitches (SK2P or SP2P) using this method by slipping one stitch over two stitches that are knitted/purled together.

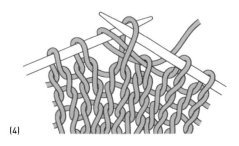

(4)

CREATING TEXTURE

Although even plain knitting has a tactile nature, there are many other exciting knitted textures to explore. Some of the most basic methods are explained here, and there are lots more in the Stitch library.

TWISTING STITCHES

Use this method to make one or more knit stitches travel across a purl stitch background. The knit stitch(es) can travel either to the left or the right. You will need a cable needle to twist more than two stitches.

◆ T2B (twist 2 back)

This method twists the knit stitch to the right. Knit into the front of the second stitch on the left-hand needle (1) (you will find it easier if you loosen the stitch with the tip of the needle first). Then purl into the front of the first stitch, transferring both stitches onto the right-hand needle.

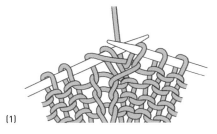

(1)

◆ T2F (twist 2 front)

This method twists the knit stitch to the left. Purl into the back of the second stitch on the left-hand needle (2). Then knit into the back of the first stitch, transferring both stitches onto the right-hand needle.

(2)

CROSSING STITCHES

Using this method, two strands of knit stitches cross each other, with a purl stitch between them when there are more than two stitches. You will need a cable needle to cross more than two stitches without dropping them.

◆ Cr2B (cross 2 back)

This crosses the right strand behind the left one. On a knit row, knit into the front of the second stitch on the left-hand needle (3). Then knit into the front of the first stitch, transferring both stitches onto the right-hand needle. On a purl row, purl the stitches instead.

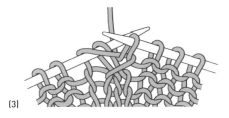

(3)

◆ Cr2F (cross 2 front)

This crosses the right strand in front of the left one. On a knit row, knit into the back of the second stitch on the left-hand needle (4). Then knit into the back of the first stitch, transferring both stitches onto the right-hand needle. On a purl row, purl the stitches instead.

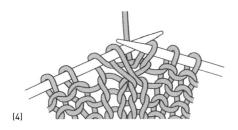

(4)

◆ Cr3B (cross 3 back)

On a knit row, slip the first two stitches (a knit, then a purl stitch) onto a cable needle and hold them at the back of the work. Knit the third stitch on the left-hand needle. Slip the second (purl stitch) back onto the left-hand needle and purl it. Knit the remaining stitch from the cable needle.

Cr3F (cross 3 front)

On a knit row, slip the first two stitches (a knit, then a purl stitch) onto a cable needle and hold them at the front of the work. Knit the third stitch on the left-hand needle. Slip the second (purl stitch) back onto the left-hand needle and purl it. Knit the remaining stitch from the cable needle.

CABLING

Cables are a distinctive feature of Aran designs, but also make simple panels or overall patterns on any knitting. Typically, two sets of two or more stitches change places to produce a ropelike pattern. You will need a cable needle.

◆ C4B (cable 4 back)

This crosses the right strand behind the left one. Slip the next two stitches onto the cable needle and hold them at the back of the work (5). Knit the next two stitches from the left-hand needle. Then knit the stitches from the cable needle.

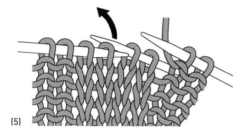

(5)

◆ C4F (cable 4 front)

This crosses the right strand in front of the left one. Slip the next two stitches onto the cable needle and hold them at the front of the work. Knit the next two stitches from the left-hand needle (6), then those from the cable needle.

(6)

ELONGATING A STITCH

You can create some interesting effects by making some stitches longer than others. Here are two methods to try.

◆ Elongated stitch

The first method forms an openwork band (see the knitted sample at the top of page 109). On the knit row, insert the tip of the right-hand needle into the next stitch. Wrap the yarn over the right-hand needle two or three times. Then finish the stitch (7). On the next row, work one stitch into each elongated stitch like an ordinary knit stitch, releasing the extra loop(s) (8).

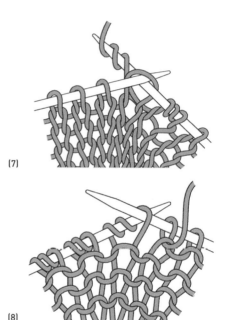

(7)

(8)

◆ sl1 (slip 1 stitch)

This forms a long vertical loop on one side of the knitting, which can be particularly effective when working with two colors (see the knitted samples on pages 211–227). Simply transfer either a knit or a purl stitch from the left- to the right-hand needle without knitting into it. Always slip a stitch purlwise unless the instruction specifically says knitwise.

KNITTING IN BEADS AND SEQUINS

Beads and sequins can be incorporated into plainer knitting to form a distinctive pattern of their own. They can also be used to embellish a knitted pattern such as lace or to form an effective trimming.

Choose beads and sequins that have holes large enough to thread the yarn through and that are not too heavy in order to avoid pulling the knitting out of shape. Sequins with one hole near the edge and seed pearl beads are ideal.

Thread the beads or sequins onto the yarn before starting to knit. First, cut a length of sewing thread, fold it in half, and thread both cut ends through the eye of a fine sewing needle. Thread a 6-inch (15-cm) end of knitting yarn through the loop in the sewing thread. Thread the required number of beads or sequins along the sewing needle and onto the yarn (9). Remember to thread the beads or sequins in reverse order if you want to follow a specific color pattern. Rewind the ball of yarn.

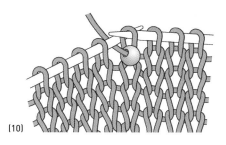

(10)

Knitting in sequins

To knit in a sequin, work up to its position in the pattern. Keep the yarn and sequin on the wrong side and push the sequin close to the last stitch. Knit the next stitch through the back loop (11), pulling the sequin through to the right side with the loop of the stitch. The sequin will hang vertically and lie flat against the knitting.

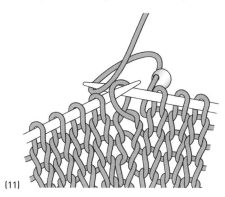

(11)

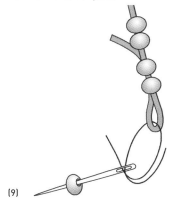

(9)

Knitting in beads

To knit in a bead, work up to its position in the pattern. Bring the yarn to the right side and push the bead along the yarn so it is close to the last stitch. Slip the next stitch. Bring the yarn to the wrong side (10) and firmly work the next stitch. The bead will then sit horizontally on the front of the work.

WORKING WITH COLOR

Using more than one color will add a new dimension to your knitting. You can be very creative just with simple stripes or by using two colors and a slip stitch to give some surprising results. Learning the techniques of stranding, weaving, and how to use bobbins will also open up the world of Fair Isle and intarsia to you.

CARRYING YARN UP THE SIDE

Sometimes you will need to change colors at the end of a row, for example when working horizontal stripes. If you are working with several different colors, each over an even number of rows, you can carry them up the side of the work instead of cutting and rejoining them. However, don't carry so many yarns up the side that they become very bulky.

When you finish with a particular color, let it hang at the end of the row while you work with a different color. Each time you return to the same edge, twist the yarns (1) and continue working with the appropriate color.

STRANDING

When two or three colors are used in one row, each color can be carried for up to five stitches across the back of the work until it is needed again. Be careful not to get the gauge too tight or it will pucker the fabric and reduce its elasticity. Spread out the stitches on the right-hand needle to keep the work elastic. Continue stranding the yarns to the end of each row to produce a double thickness of fabric and twist the strands at the end of each row for a neat finish.

Stranding with one hand

This method is the same for knit and purl rows. Work up to the color change and insert the tip of the right-hand needle into the next stitch. Drop the first color, pick up the second one, and work the next stitches according to the pattern. Continue to change colors in this way.

Stranding with two hands

On a knit row, knit up to the color change with the yarn in the right hand while holding the other yarn away from the needles with the left hand (2). Then knit the next batch of stitches in the contrast color with the left hand (see page 22), again holding the other yarn away from the needles (3).

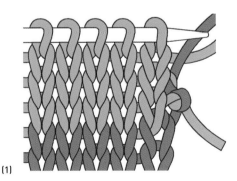

(1)

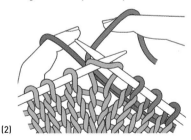

(2)

(3)

> **TIP** If you are knitting odd rows of color, the yarn will be at the wrong end of the row when you need to use it again. Knit on two double-pointed needles or back and forth on a circular needle. When you use the yarn again, purl instead of knit or knit instead of purl the row, working the stitches from the chart appropriately.

On a purl row, first work with the yarn in the right hand as usual but hold the second yarn forward and away from the needles with the left hand (4). To change colors, purl the next stitches with the contrast color, using the left thumb and index finger and holding the first yarn away from the needles with the right hand (5).

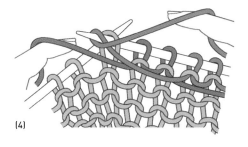

(4)

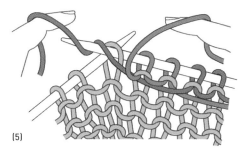

(5)

WEAVING

When working with two colors that need to be carried across more than five stitches, it is best to weave them. Do this every three to four stitches so that the unworked yarns are not long enough to snag and the gauge stays even. Always weave the yarns in different positions on each row so that the woven yarns do not show through and ridges do not form. Although weaving also produces a double thickness of fabric, it is less elastic than one that has been stranded.

Weaving with two hands

This method is quicker using both hands, but can be adapted to one.

On a knit row, work with the main color in the right hand. Insert the tip of the right-hand needle into the next stitch. Holding the contrast color in the left hand (see page 22), carry it under the main color and over the top of the tip of the right-hand needle from back to front (6). Knit the stitch with the main color (7), at the same time drawing the new stitch under the loop of contrast color so that the loop falls off the right-hand needle. Hold down the contrast color with the left thumb so that it is woven in when you work the next stitch with the main color.

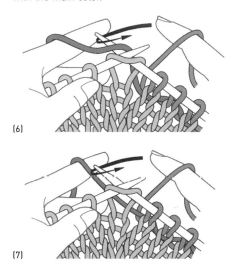

(6)

(7)

On a purl row, hold the main and contrast colors as for knit rows. Insert the right-hand needle purlwise into the next stitch and bring the contrast color over the top of the right-hand needle from front to back (8). Purl the stitch with the main color, drawing the new stitch under the loop of contrast color so that the loop falls off the right-hand needle (9). Hold down the contrast color for the next stitch to continue weaving it in.

a 4-inch (10-cm) end for weaving in later. Knit the required number of stitches in the second color and then leave the bobbin hanging on a short length of yarn at the back of the work. Introduce the next color in the same way.

On subsequent rows, introduce any new colors as before. However, before changing from one existing color to another, twist one yarn over the other (10, 11). This forms a link between the separate blocks of color, preventing holes.

As you finish work with each color for the last time, cut the yarn, leaving a 4-inch (10-cm) end so that it can be woven in later.

(8)

(9)

WORKING BLOCKS OF COLOR

When blocks of two or more colors are worked in the same row, for example for vertical stripes, multicolored patterns, or intarsia motifs, carrying the yarn across the back of the work would cause unsightly bunching and uneven gauge. Instead, wind a quantity of each of the colored yarns you need around a bobbin before starting to knit.

Twisting yarns

Start knitting with the color required in the pattern. When you reach the position for the next color, knit the first stitch in that new color, leaving

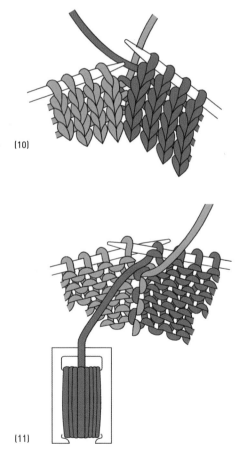

(10)

(11)

MAKING SELVAGES

Keep the side edges of your knitting neat by knitting a selvage. A one-stitch selvage is easier to seam or to pick up stitches. A two-stitch selvage forms a decorative edge where there is no other finish. You may need to add extra stitches to form the selvage so that the pattern will flow across the seam uninterrupted.

SINGLE STOCKINETTE STITCH EDGE
Use this selvage where seams are to be joined edge-to-edge or you need to pick up stitches (1). On right side rows, slip the first stitch knitwise and then knit to the end of the row in the usual way. On wrong side rows, slip the first stitch purlwise and then purl to the end.

SINGLE GARTER STITCH EDGE
This forms a flat edge for garter stitch (2). On every row, slip the first stitch purlwise. Then bring the yarn to the back of the work and knit to the end of the row.

SINGLE SEED STITCH EDGE
This selvage forms a firm border for stockinette stitch and a firm edge for seams (3). Knit the first and last stitches of every row.

DOUBLE GARTER STITCH EDGE
This firm, even selvage will not curl up (4). On every row, slip the first stitch knitwise, knit the second stitch, and then work to the end of the row, knitting the last two stitches.

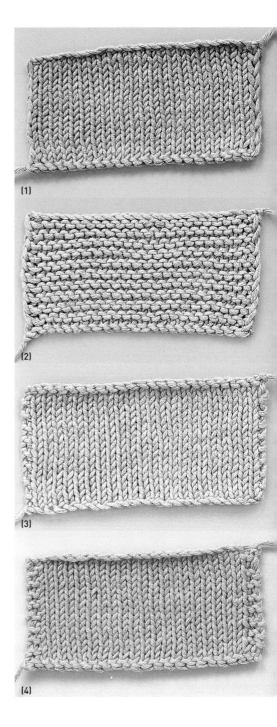

(1)

(2)

(3)

(4)

CORRECTING MISTAKES

Remember to check your knitting after every few rows to make sure that you have not made any mistakes. It is always much easier to correct a mistake sooner rather than later, and without necessarily unraveling too much of your knitting.

UNRAVELING ONE ROW

Keep all the stitches on the needles. On a knit row, insert the tip of the left-hand needle, from front to back, into the stitch below the first stitch on the right-hand needle.

On a purl row, insert the left-hand needle from back to front. Pull out the right-hand needle, releasing the yarn from the top stitch and transferring the one below to the left-hand needle (1). Continue unraveling stitches until you can rework the stitches correctly.

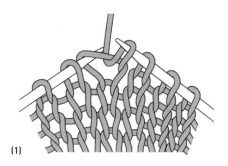

(1)

PICKING UP DROPPED STITCHES

For each of these methods, first unravel the stitches on the last row or work the next row until you reach the position of the dropped stitch, keeping all the stitches on the needles.

Picking up one knit stitch

Hold the work with the knit side facing you. Insert the tip of the right-hand needle into the dropped stitch from front to back and then under the horizontal strand of yarn above it. Insert the tip of the left-hand needle into the dropped stitch from back to front and bring it over the horizontal

strand and off the right-hand needle (2). Transfer the corrected stitch to the left-hand needle and continue knitting.

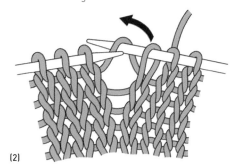

(2)

Picking up one purl stitch

Hold the work with the purl side facing you. Insert the tip of the right-hand needle through the dropped stitch from back to front and then pick up the horizontal strand of yarn above it. Insert the tip of the left-hand needle into the dropped stitch from front to back and bring it over the horizontal strand and off the right-hand needle (3). Transfer the stitch to the left-hand needle and continue.

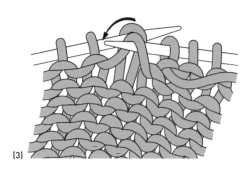

(3)

Picking up a running stitch

A running stitch is a stitch that has been dropped more than one row below. The following technique is easiest to do on plain stockinette stitch but can be adapted for other simple patterns. If you have dropped a stitch a few rows down, you can correct it this way. Only use this technique to pick up a running stitch over four or five rows. It is better to unravel and rework the knitting over more rows to avoid the gauge from becoming uneven.

Keep the stitches on the needles but slide them away from the tips to create a "ladder". Lay the knitting flat, with the knit side facing you. Insert a crochet hook through the running stitch and under the first horizontal strand of yarn above (4). Turn the hook slightly and pull the strand through the stitch. Continue picking up the stitches to the top of the ladder and transfer the last one to the left-hand needle.

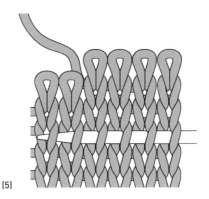

(5)

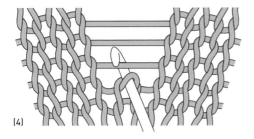

(4)

UNRAVELING SEVERAL ROWS

Take the work off the needles and gather it into one hand. Carefully unravel each row down to the one above the row with the mistake. Replace the knitting on a needle and unravel the final row as explained on page 34.

CORRECTING COMPLEX PATTERNS

To correct a mistake neatly in complex lace, cable, or color patterns, it is often quicker and easier to unravel the relevant rows. However, there are a few techniques that can help in the appropriate circumstances.

Picking up the row below

Thread a thinner needle through the first loop in each stitch right across a row below the one with the mistake, picking a row without too much patterning so that you can see the stitches clearly. Unravel the work above the spare needle (5). Replace the work on the correct needle, making sure each stitch faces the correct direction, ready to begin knitting again.

Correcting color patterns

If you have worked a whole row or more incorrectly, you could use the grafting method to correct the mistake.

Thread one thinner needle through the stitches in the row below the mistake and another in the row above. Then cut the yarns in the middle of the incorrect row(s) and unravel the yarn so that you have two pieces of knitting. Reknit any missing rows, except the last one, onto the bottom piece.

Lay the two pieces together. Thread a tapestry needle with the correct color of yarn to start the remaining missing row. Bring the needle from back to front through the loop of the first knitted stitch on the bottom piece. Insert it across the loops at the bottom of the first knitted stitch on the top piece and then back down through the loop of the first stitch on the bottom piece.

Continue making each stitch in this way, changing the colors as necessary and keeping the gauge even, until you have finished the row. Weave in the loose yarn ends later.

TIP When you run out of yarn, don't start a new ball in the middle of a row, whether it's the same or a different color. Always start a new ball at the seam edge. Work a few stitches with the new yarn and then knot the old and new yarn ends together at the edge. When you have finished knitting, undo the knot and weave the ends into the seam as usual (see page 36).

FINISHING

Take the time and care to finish your knitting well for a really professional look. First you will need to weave in any yarn ends and block and/or press the knitting. If you are making a garment, you will sew the pieces together and then pick up new stitches to knit on other parts, such as a neck band. You will find all these methods on the next few pages.

WEAVING IN ENDS

Most yarn ends will be at the side edges. Thread the loose end into a tapestry needle. Weave the thread into the seam edge for about 2 inches (5 cm) (1), keeping the tension elastic. Trim the excess.

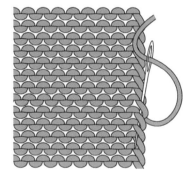

(1)

It's not a good idea to join new yarn in the middle of a row, so you should only have ends left there when knitting intarsia. Carefully weave the yarn over and through the purl loops on the back of the knitting so that it does not show at the front (2). Make sure to keep the tension elastic and try to weave the yarn across an area of the same color.

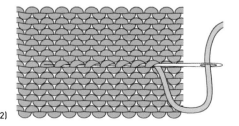

(2)

BLOCKING AND PRESSING

Always consult the yarn label before blocking or pressing a particular yarn. If this is not available, experiment on a gauge swatch first. Blocking and pressing are particularly suitable for stockinette stitch to smooth out any stitch irregularities. However, most synthetic yarns would be ruined by either process, and ribbing would lose its elasticity. You can block highly textured knitting such as cable or lace patterns, but you should not press it.

Blocking

Blocking allows you to shape pieces of knitting to the correct dimensions. Lay a sheet of plastic on a large, flat surface, then a folded blanket or a few thick towels and an old sheet on top. Pin the knitting, right side up, onto the surface. Use rust-proof straight or dressmaking pins and place them at key points. Check that the rows and stitches run in straight lines and the knitting is laid out to the correct dimensions. Continue pinning at intervals of about 2 inches (5 cm)—closer around curves—to keep the edges from curling (3). Don't stretch the

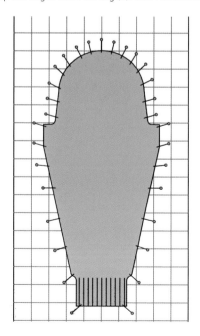

(3)

fabric, although lacy patterns do benefit from being opened out. Do not pin around ribbing. Lightly spray the knitting with cold water. Allow the pieces to air-dry thoroughly, away from direct heat.

Pressing

Lay the knitting, right side down, on a flat, padded surface. Use rust-proof straight pins with small metal heads to pin down the knitting, placing the pins at an angle and pushing them well into the padding. Do not pin down, or press, ribbing.

Place a clean cotton press cloth over the knitting. For natural fibers, use a damp cloth and a steam iron set at the appropriate temperature for the fiber. Use a cool iron and dry cloth on any synthetic-natural fiber blends suitable for pressing. Apply the iron briefly and very lightly to the cloth. Then lift, rather than slide, it and reapply it to another area.

Steaming, rather than pressing, is appropriate for some fibers such as mohair and angora, and for textured stitches. Use a damp cloth and hold a moderately hot steam iron just above the cloth for a moment to create steam.

PICKING UP NEW STITCHES

You will need to pick up new stitches along the edge of your knitting to make borders such as button and neck bands. To pick them up evenly, insert pins at regular intervals along the edge to help you knit the correct number of stitches between markers (4).

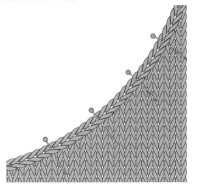

(4)

TIP As a general rule, pick up three stitches for every four rows along a straight edge of stockinette stitch.

With the right side facing and using a smaller needle than for the rest of your knitting, insert the tip through a stitch in the existing piece of knitting. Wrap yarn from a new ball knitwise around the needle and pull the loop through and onto the needle. Continue to pick up the required number of stitches in the same way.

Along a vertical edge such as a button band, make the first new stitch between the first and second stitches on the first row (5). Make subsequent stitches directly above it.

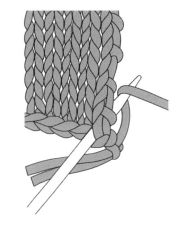

(5)

On a bound-off edge such as the front of a neckline, insert the needle through the center of the stitches one row below the bound-off edge (6).

(6)

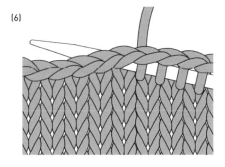

Make sure to produce a smooth line of stitches and to avoid holes from forming. For example, you could pick up a few more stitches around a neck edge than are actually required and then decrease them again as you work the first row of ribbing.

MAKING BUTTONHOLES

Buttonholes form a handy fastening that you can easily incorporate as you knit. The sturdiest are bound-off buttonholes. They are often worked horizontally on a separate vertical band but will fall vertically on a band that is picked up along a front edge.

With the right side facing, work up to the buttonhole. Bind off the appropriate number of stitches (often two or four, depending on the yarn and button size) (7). Work to the end of the row.

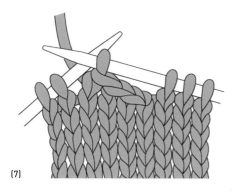

(7)

On the next row, work up to the bound-off stitches. Cast on the same number using the single cast-on method (8). Work to the end.

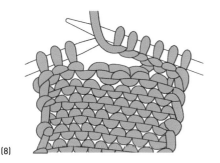

(8)

TIP You can make small buttonholes for baby's garments using a yarn-over increase to make a single eyelet on the first row and knitting two stitches together on the next row.

SEWING UP

Neatly joined, elastic seams are vital to a garment that is practical and a pleasure to wear. You can sew or graft seams together.

Use a tapestry needle and an 8-inch (20-cm) length of the knitting yarn. If that yarn is too uneven or easily broken, use a matching smooth yarn of the same fiber content. Sew in the loose ends after the seam is finished.

Mattress stitch

This stitch produces smooth, invisible seams such as side seams.

Lay the pieces to be joined right side up and side by side on a flat surface. Leaving a short end of yarn, insert the needle between the first and second knitted stitches on the first row of a vertical edge or through the center of the first knitted stitch on a bound-off edge. Insert the needle under two rows if the knit side, and under one row if the purl side, on the right side. Insert the needle at the same place on the other edge to be joined. Bring it out two rows above. Insert the needle where it last emerged on the first edge and bring the needle out two rows above (9).

Continue for about 3/4 inch (2 cm). Pull the thread up very tightly to close the seam and then stretch the seam slightly to maintain its elasticity.

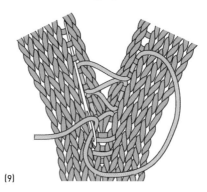

(9)

Back stitch

Back stitch can be useful for seams where there are different numbers of stitches in each piece, such as around an armhole or along a shoulder that has been bound off on different rows.

Place the pieces right sides together. Leaving a short end of yarn, insert the needle down through the knitting and back up two knitted stitches along the edge to the left. Take the needle down again one knitted stitch to the right (10). Continue, keeping the back stitches one knitted stitch in from the edge and the wrong side as neat as on the right side.

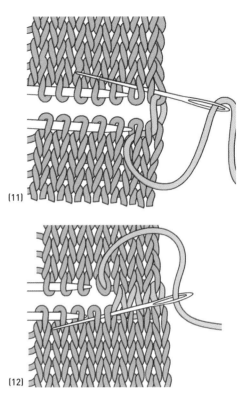

(11)

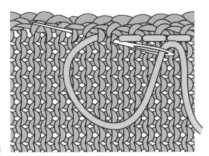

(10)

Grafting

This way of weaving two sets of stitches together also produces an invisible seam and can only be used when each piece has the same number of stitches, such as for a shoulder seam. Grafting is not suitable when a heavy yarn would weigh down a sleeve and stretch the seam.

Keeping the work on knitting needles, either hold both pieces in the left hand with the wrong sides together or lay them right sides up and edge to edge on a flat surface.

For stockinette stitch, insert the tapestry needle from back to front through the first knitted stitch on each piece. Insert it again down through the first knitted stitch on the bottom piece and up through the next knitted stitch on the same piece (11). Repeat this on the top piece. Continue joining pairs of stitches in this way to the end of the seam (12).

(12)

For garter stitch, bring the tapestry needle up through the first knitted stitches on each piece as for stockinette stitch. Then insert it again down through the next knitted stitch on the top piece and the first stitch on the bottom piece. Repeat the steps to complete the seam.

CARING FOR KNITWEAR

After you have spent hours knitting a garment or home furnishing, you will be looking forward to enjoying it for many years. The appropriate care will ensure that your knitting retains its original color, texture, and shape.

LAUNDERING

Many yarns are machine washable, and you will usually find care instructions on the yarn label. If you are in any doubt, it is always best to hand wash an item unless specifically advised not to.

Turn a garment inside out before hand washing it with soap powder or mild detergent in cool to lukewarm water. Don't rub the knitted item, but instead gently lift and submerge it to work up a lather. Use two or three rinses of clean water to get rid of all the soap. Never wring the item but, supporting its weight with both hands, gently squeeze out as much water as possible. Spin the item or roll it in a clean towel to soak up excess water. Never tumble dry wool.

Lay the item out on a flat, colorfast surface, gently easing it into shape. Leave it to air-dry away from direct heat or sunlight. When it is completely dry, you could hang it outdoors, fastening it with clothespins in an inconspicuous place such as under the arms.

Follow the instructions on the yarn label for machine washing and dry-cleaning. Turn a garment inside out before putting it in the machine. You could also put it in a pillowcase to keep it from stretching too much. Take the item out of the machine promptly after the wash to minimize creasing. Dry it flat, easing it into shape, as for hand washing.

If a knitted item has been shaped while drying, it shouldn't need pressing. However, if it does, consult the yarn label and page 37.

STORING

Never hang a knitted garment up because its weight will pull it out of shape. Instead, fold it and store it in a drawer or on a shelf. To store an item for a period of time, put it in a plastic bag or container with a natural moth repellent.

MAKING MINOR REPAIRS

Always keep leftover yarn and one or two spare buttons so that you can easily make minor repairs.

If a knitted garment snags, don't trim the pulled yarn, as a hole will quickly develop. Instead, ease each stitch back to its correct size with a tapestry needle, working from the pulled loop to each end of the snag.

If the yarn pills over time, gently pull off the tiny balls of fluff or lightly apply adhesive tape to pull them off.

Repair small holes immediately to stop them from growing. Using a tapestry needle, bring a matching length of yarn up through the loop of the first stitch at the right-hand end of the hole. Weave the yarn alternately through the top and bottom loops to simulate each missing knitted stitch. To finish, weave the loose yarn ends in at the back.

CARE INSTRUCTION SYMBOLS

WASHING

The temperatures in the basins indicate the recommended initial water temperatures for each type of washing action. Be sure to check the yarn label for the manufacturer's recommended water temperature.

Normal wash (no bar)
Yarn withstands normal washing action at quoted washtub temperature

Permanent press wash (single bar)
Yarn withstands reduced washing action at quoted washtub temperature

Gentle or delicate wash (double bar)
Yarn withstands much reduced washing action at quoted washtub temperature

Hand wash only
Do not machine wash

TUMBLE DRYING

Can be tumble dried

Can be tumble dried on low setting

Can be tumble dried on medium setting

Do not tumble dry

PRESSING

Hot iron

Warm iron

Cool iron

Do not iron

DRY CLEANING

Different letters in the circle indicate to the dry cleaner the fluid that can be used

Can be dry-cleaned

Do not dry-clean

BLEACHING

Chlorine bleach can be used

Do not use chlorine bleach

DRYING

Dry flat

Line dry

Stitch library

This collection presents more than
300 stitch patterns to tempt even
experienced knitters, although many of
them are easy to knit. They include
subtle textures, intriguing textures, and
fun, chunky textures; there are stitches
that look best in one color and patterns
for multicolors; there are Aran, lace, and
Fair Isle stitches—just take your pick!

Knit and purl patterns

The basic stitches—knit and purl—can be combined to produce an amazing variety of patterns and textures all on their own. The most commonly used, shown on this spread, also provide the backgrounds so essential to set off lace, cables, and other textured stitches to their best advantage.

This section presents a taste of the hundreds of stitch patterns that have been devised over the generations. Some of their names are well known; others may differ from region to region. Intriguingly, most hint at their visual associations or their possible origins.

Select a plain, smooth, single-colored yarn and use a fairly tight gauge to make the most of these stitch patterns, whether you choose the scattered interest of Simple Seed Texture stitch, the satisfying depth of Moss stitch, or the bulky texture of Mosaic stitch.

STOCKINETTE stitch
Any number of sts
Row 1: (RS) K.
Row 2: P.
Rep these 2 rows.

REVERSE STOCKINETTE stitch
Any number of sts
Row 1: (RS) P.
Row 2: K.
Rep these 2 rows.

GARTER stitch (reversible)
Any number of sts
Every row: K.

STOCKINETTE stitch (top section of picture)
REVERSE STOCKINETTE stitch (middle section of picture)
GARTER stitch (bottom section of picture)

SIMPLE SEED TEXTURE stitch

Multiples of 4 sts plus 1
Row 1: (RS) P1, *K3, P1, rep from * to end.
Row 2: P.
Row 3: K.
Row 4: P.
Row 5: K2, P1, *K3, P1, rep from * to last 2 sts, K2.
Row 6: P.
Row 7: K.
Row 8: P.
Rep these 8 rows.

DIAMOND brocade

Multiples of 12 sts plus 1
Row 1: (RS) *K1, P1, K9, P1, rep from * to last st, K1.
Row 2: K1, *P1, K1, P7, K1, P1, K1, rep from * to end.
Row 3: *(K1, P1) twice, K5, P1, K1, P1, rep from * to last st, K1.
Row 4: K1, *(P1, K1) twice, P3, K1, P1, K1, P2, rep from * to end.
Row 5: *K3, P1, (K1, P1) 3 times, K2, rep from * to last st, K1.
Row 6: P1, *P3, K1, (P1, K1) twice, P4, rep from * to end.
Row 7: *K5, P1, K1, P1, K4, rep from * to last st, K1.
Row 8: As row 6.
Row 9: As row 5.
Row 10: As row 4.
Row 11: As row 3.
Row 12: K1, *P1, K1, P7, K1, P1, K1, rep from * to end.
Rep these 12 rows.

BASIC SEED stitch (BRITISH or IRISH MOSS stitch) (reversible)

Multiples of 2 sts
Row 1: *K1, P1, rep from * to end.
Row 2: *P1, K1, rep from * to end.
Rep these 2 rows.

Multiples of 2 sts plus 1
Row 1: K1, *P1, K1, rep from * to end.
Row 2: P1, *K1, P1, rep from * to end.
Rep these 2 rows.

DOUBLE MOSS stitch (reversible)

Multiples of 4 sts plus 2
Row 1: *K2, P2, rep from * to last 2 sts, K2.
Row 2: *P2, K2, rep from * to last 2 sts, P2.
Row 3: As row 2.
Row 4: As row 1.
Rep these 4 rows.

CHEVRON SEED stitch

Multiples of 8 sts
Row 1: (RS) *P1, K3, rep from * to end.
Row 2: *K1, P5, K1, P1, rep from * to end.
Row 3: *K2, P1, K3, P1, K1, rep from * to end.
Row 4: *P2, K1, P1, K1, P3, rep from * to end.
Rep these 4 rows.

DEEP CHEVRON pattern (reversible)

Multiples of 12 sts
Row 1: *K3, P5, K3, P1, rep from * to end.
Row 2: *K1, P3, K5, P3, rep from * to end.
Row 3: P1, *K3, P3, rep from * to last 5 sts, K3, P2.
Row 4: K2, P3, *K3, P3, rep from * to last st, K1.
Row 5: *P2, K3, P1, K3, P3, rep from * to end.
Row 6: *K3, P3, K1, P3, K2, rep from * to end.
Row 7: *P3, K5, P3, K1, rep from * to end.
Row 8: *P1, K3, P5, K3, rep from * to end.
Row 9: K1, *P3, K3, rep from * to last 5 sts, P3, K2.
Row 10: P2, K3, *P3, K3, rep from * to last st, P1.
Row 11: *K2, P3, K1, P3, K3, rep from * to end.
Row 12: *P3, K3, P1, K3, P2, rep from * to end.
Rep these 12 rows.

DOUBLE MOSS stitch (top section of picture)
CHEVRON SEED stitch (middle section of picture)
DEEP CHEVRON pattern (bottom section of picture)

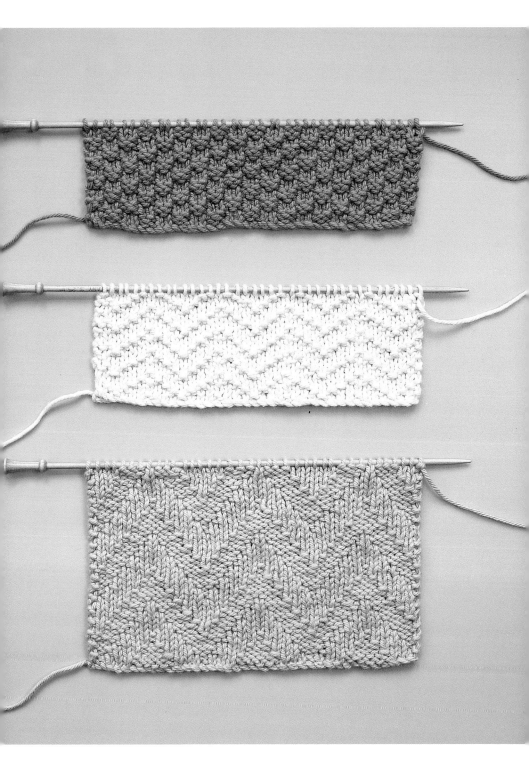

DIAGONAL SEED stitch
Multiples of 5 sts
Row 1: (RS) *K4, P1, rep from * to end.
Row 2: *P1, K1, P3, rep from * to end.
Row 3: *K2, P1, K2, rep from * to end.
Row 4: *P3, K1, P1, rep from * to end.
Row 5: *P1, K4, rep from * to end.
Row 6: *K1, P4, rep from * to end.
Row 7: *K3, P1, K1, rep from * to end.
Row 8: *P2, K1, P2, rep from * to end.
Row 9: *K1, P1, K3, rep from * to end.
Row 10: *P4, K1, rep from * to end.
Rep these 10 rows.

TIP Diagonal patterns tend to stretch on the bias. To minimize this, choose firmly twisted yarns, not soft ones, and don't wring the fabric when washing it.

RIB checkerboard
Multiples of 13 sts
Row 1: (RS) *K5, (P1, K1) 4 times, rep from * to end.
Row 2: *(P1, K1) 4 times, P5, rep from * to end.
Rows 3, 5, and 7: As row 1.
Rows 4, 6, and 8: As row 2.
Row 9: *(K1, P1) 4 times, K5, rep from * to end.
Row 10: *P5, (KI, P1) 4 times, rep from * to end.
Rows 11, 13, and 15: As row 1.
Rows 12, 14, and 16: As row 2.
Rep these 16 rows.

MOSS stitch (reversible)
Multiples of 2 sts
Row 1: *K1, P1, rep from * to end.
Row 2: As row 1.
Row 3: *P1, K1, rep from * to end.
Row 4: As row 3.
Rep these 4 rows.

Multiples of 2 sts plus 1
Row 1: *K1, P1, rep from * to last st, K1.
Row 2: *P1, K1, rep from * to last st, P1.
Row 3: As row 2.
Row 4: As row 1.
Rep these 4 rows.

DIAGONAL SEED stitch (top section of picture)
RIB checkerboard (middle section of picture)
MOSS stitch (bottom section of picture)

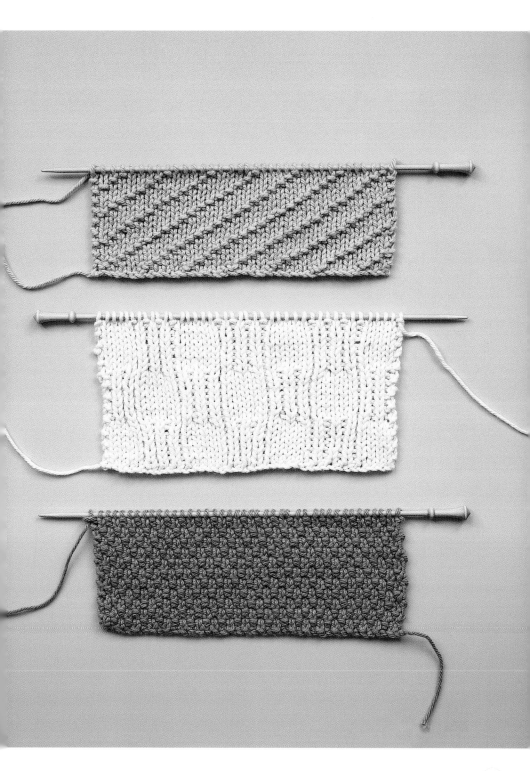

LITTLE ARROW stitch

Multiples of 8 sts plus 1

Row 1: (RS) K2, P2, K1, P2, *K3, P2, K1, P2, rep from * to last 2 sts, K2.

Row 2: P3, K1, P1, K1, *P5, K1, P1, K1, rep from * to last 3 sts, P3.

Row 3: K1, *P1, K5, P1, K1, rep from * to end.

Row 4: P1, *K2, P3, K2, P1, rep from * to end.

Rep these 4 rows.

DIAMOND SEED brocade

Multiples of 8 sts

Row 1: (RS) *P1, K7, rep from * to end.

Row 2: *K1, P5, K1, P1, rep from * to end.

Row 3: *K2, P1, K3, P1, K1, rep from * to end.

Row 4: *P2, K1, P1, K1, P3, rep from * to end.

Row 5: *K4, P1, K3, rep from * to end.

Row 6: As row 4.

Row 7: As row 3.

Row 8: As row 2.

Rep these 8 rows.

FOUR-STITCH check (reversible)

Multiples of 8 sts

Rows 1, 2, and 3: *K4, P4, rep from * to end.

Rows 4, 5, and 6: *P4, K4, rep from * to end.

Rep these 6 rows.

LITTLE ARROW stitch (top section of picture)
DIAMOND SEED brocade (middle section of picture)
FOUR-STITCH check (bottom section of picture)

HORIZONTAL DASH stitch

Multiples of 10 sts

Row 1: (RS) *K4, P6, rep from *
to end.

Row 2 and all WS rows: P.

Row 3: K.

Row 5: *P5, K4, P1, rep from *
to end.

Row 7: K.

Row 8: P.

Rep these 8 rows.

STOCKINETTE STITCH check

Multiples of 8 sts

Row 1: (RS) *P2, K4, rep from *
to end.

Row 2: P.

Row 3: As row 1.

Row 4: P.

Row 5: K3, *P2, K4, rep from *
to last 3 sts, P2, K1.

Row 6: P.

Row 7: As row 5.

Row 8: P.

Rep these 8 rows.

BASKET stitch

Multiples of 6 sts

Row 1: (RS) K.

Row 2: P.

Row 3: *K1, P4, K1, rep from *
to end.

Row 4: *P1, K4, P1, rep from *
to end.

Row 5: As row 3.

Row 6: As row 4.

Row 7: K.

Row 8: P.

Row 9: *P2, K2, P2, rep from *
to end.

Row 10: *K2, P2, K2, rep from *
to end.

Row 11: As row 9.

Row 12: As row 10.

Rep these 12 rows.

HORIZONTAL DASH stitch (top section of picture)
STOCKINETTE STITCH check (middle section of picture)
BASKET stitch (bottom section of picture)

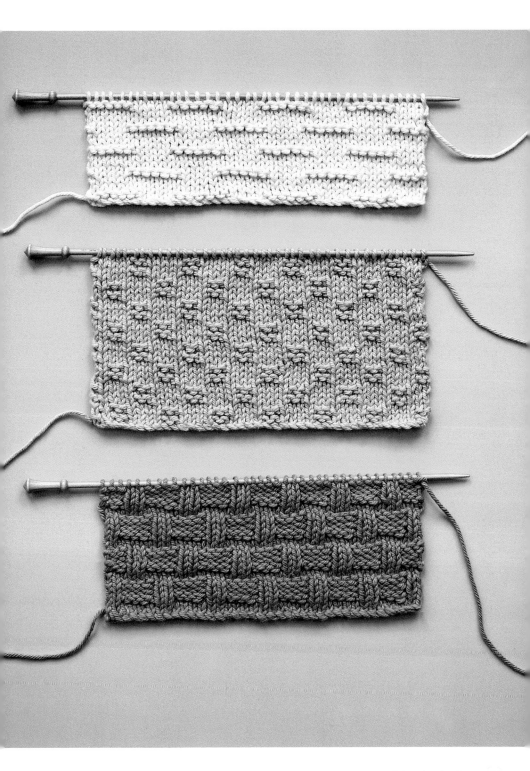

ANDALUSIAN stitch

Multiples of 2 sts
Row 1: (RS) K.
Row 2: P.
Row 3: *K1, P1, rep from *
to end.
Row 4: P.
Rep these 4 rows.

WAVED WELT stitch (reversible)

Multiples of 8 sts plus 1
Row 1: (RS) *P1, K7, rep from *
to last st, P1.
Row 2: K2,*P5, K3, rep from *
to last 7 sts, P5, K2.
Row 3: P3, *K3, P5, rep from *
to last 6 sts, K3, P3.
Row 4: K4, *P1, K7, rep from *
to last 5 sts, P1, K4.
Row 5: *K1, P7, rep from * to
last st, K1.
Row 6: P2, *K5, P3, rep from *
to last 7 sts, K5, P2.
Row 7: K3, *P3, K5, rep from *
to last 6 sts, P3, K3.
Row 8: P4, *K1, P7, rep from *
to last 5 sts, K1, P4.
Rep these 8 rows.

PENNANT stitch

Multiples of 5 sts
Row 1: (RS) K.
Row 2: *K1, P4, rep from *
to end.
Row 3: *K3, P2, rep from *
to end.
Row 4: As row 3.
Row 5: As row 2.
Row 6: K.
Rep these 6 rows.

ANDALUSIAN stitch (top section of picture)
WAVED WELT stitch (middle section of picture)
PENNANT stitch (bottom section of picture)

PYRAMID stitch

Multiples of 8 sts plus 1

Row 1: (RS) *K1, P7, rep from * to last st, K1.
Row 2: P1, *K7, P1, rep from * to end.
Row 3: *K2, P5, K1, rep from * to last st, K1.
Row 4: P1, *P1, K5, P2, rep from * to end.
Row 5: *K3, P3, K2, rep from * to last st, K1.
Row 6: P1, *P2, K3, P3, rep from * to end.
Row 7: *K4, P1, K3, rep from * to last st, K1.
Row 8: P1, *P3, K1, P4, rep from * to end.
Row 9: *P4, K1, P3, rep from * to last st, P1.
Row 10: K1, *K3, P1, K4, rep from * to end.
Row 11: *P3, K3, P2, rep from * to last st, P1.
Row 12: K1, *K2, P3, K3, rep from * to end.
Row 13: *P2, K5, P1, rep from * to last st, P1.
Row 14: K1, *K1, P5, K2, rep from * to end.
Row 15: *P1, K7, rep from * to last st, P1.
Row 16: K1, *P7, K1, rep from * to end.
Rep these 16 rows.

SEEDED check

Multiples of 10 sts plus 5

Row 1: (RS) *K5, (P1, K1) twice, P1, rep from * to last 5 sts, K5.
Row 2: P5, *(P1, K1) twice, P6, rep from * to end.
Rows 3 and 5: As row 1.
Rows 4 and 6: As row 2.
Row 7: *(K1, P1) twice, K1, P5, rep from * to last 5 sts, (K1, P1) twice, K1.
Row 8: *(K1, P1) twice, K6, rep from * to last 5 sts, (K1, P1) twice, K1.
Row 9: As row 1.
Row 10: As row 2.
Row 11: As row 1.
Row 12: As row 2.
Rep these 12 rows.

MOSAIC stitch

Multiples of 20 sts plus 10

Row 1: (RS) *P2, K2, rep from * to last 2 sts, P2.
Row 2: *K2, P2, rep from * to last 2 sts, K2.
Row 3: (K2, P2) twice, *K4, P2, K2, P2, rep from * to last 2 sts, K2.
Row 4: (P2, K2) twice, *P4, K2, P2, K2, rep from * to last 2 sts, P2.
Rows 5–8: Rep rows 1–4.
Rows 9 and 10: Rep rows 1–2.
Row 11: As row 2.
Row 12: As row 1.
Row 13: As row 3.
Row 14: As row 4.
Rows 15–18: Rep rows 11–14.
Rows 19 and 20: Rep rows 11–12.
Rep these 20 rows.

PYRAMID stitch (top section of picture)
SEEDED check (middle section of picture)
MOSAIC stitch (bottom section of picture)

VERTICAL CATERPILLAR stitch

Multiples of 6 sts plus 2
Row 1: (RS) P2, *K1, P5, rep from * to end.
Row 2: K5, P1, rep from * to last 2 sts, K2.
Row 3: As row 1.
Row 4: As row 2.
Row 5: As row 1.
Row 6: As row 2.
Row 7: *P5, K1, rep from * to last 2 sts, K2.
Row 8: K2, *P1, K5, rep from * to end.
Row 9: As row 7.
Row 10: As row 8.
Row 11: As row 7.
Row 12: As row 8.
Rep these 12 rows.

HARRIS TWEED stitch (reversible)

Multiples of 4 sts
Row 1: *K2, P2, rep from * to end.
Row 2: As row 1.
Row 3: K.
Row 4: P.
Rows 5 and 6: As row 1.
Row 7: P.
Row 8: K.
Rep these 8 rows.

DIAMOND SEED stitch

Multiples of 6 sts
Row 1: (RS) *K1, P1, K4, rep from * to end.
Row 2: *P4, K1, P1, rep from * to end.
Row 3: *P1, K1, P1, K3, rep from * to end.
Row 4: *P3, K1, P1, K1, rep from * to end.
Row 5: As row 1.
Row 6: As row 2.
Row 7: *K4, P1, K1, rep from * to end.
Row 8: *P1, K1, P4, rep from * to end.
Row 9: *K3, P1, K1, P1, rep from * to end.
Row 10: *K1, P1, K1, P3, rep from * to end.
Row 11: As row 7.
Row 12: As row 8.
Rep these 12 rows.

VERTICAL CATERPILLAR stitch (top section of picture)
HARRIS TWEED stitch (middle section of picture)
DIAMOND SEED stitch (bottom section of picture)

Knit and purl panels

Knit and purl stitches easily combine to make the vertical panels so typical of the durable gansey, the traditional working garment of nineteenth-century British fishermen. Originally evolved in fishing communities along the coastlines from the Channel Islands and up the east coast of Britain to Scotland, the gansey stitch patterns are now internationally valued. The Tree of Life and Basic Seed stitch panels on the sample opposite demonstrate how just two stitch patterns create a beautiful effect.

These stitch patterns were originally passed on from one knitter to another without being formally recorded. They were often inspired by everyday objects such as fishing nets, anchors, herringbones, and lightning, although patterns such as the Tree of Life and Marriage Lines have more symbolic connotations.

Traditionally, ganseys were closely knitted, to keep out the elements, in navy blue worsted wool. Today, many plain wool and cotton yarns display the stitch patterns well, and denim cotton is a popular choice.

BASIC SEED STITCH (BRITISH or IRISH MOSS STITCH) panel (reversible)
Multiples of 2 sts
Row 1: *K1, P1, rep from * to end.
Row 2: *P1, K1, rep from * to end.
Rep these 2 rows.

Multiples of 2 sts plus 1
Row 1: *K1, P1, rep from * to last st, K1.
Rep this row.

TREE OF LIFE panel
Panel of 17 sts on St st background
Row 1: (RS) K6, P2, K1, P2, K6.
Row 2: P5, K2, P3, K2, P5.
Row 3: K4, P2, (K1, P1) twice, K1, P2, K4.
Row 4: P3, (K2, P1) 3 times, K2, P3.
Row 5: K2, P2, K1, P2, K3, P2, K1, P2, K2.
Row 6: P1, (K2, P1) twice, K1, P1, K1, (P1, K2) twice, P1.
Row 7: (P2, K1) 5 times, P2.
Row 8: K1, (P1, K2) twice, P3, (K2, P1) twice, K1.
Row 9: K1, (P2, K1) twice, P1, K1, P1, (K1, P2) twice, K1.
Row 10: P1, K1, (P1, K2) 4 times, P1, K1, P1.
Row 11: As row 5.
Row 12: P2, K1, P1, K2, (P1, K1) twice, P1, K2, P1, K1, P2.
Row 13: K3, (P2, K1) 3 times, P2, K3.
Row 14: P3, K1, P1, K2, P3, K2, P1, K1, P3.
Row 15: As row 3.
Row 16: P4, K1, (P1, K2) twice, P1, K1, P4.
Row 17: K5, P2, K3, P2, K5.
Row 18: P5, (K1, P1) 3 times, K1, P5.
Row 19: As row 1.
Row 20: P6, K1, P3, K1, P6.
Row 21: K7, P1, K1, P1, K7.
Row 22: P7, K1, K1, P7.
Rep these 22 rows.

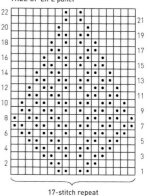

TREE OF LIFE panel

17-stitch repeat

KEY

K on RS rows, P on WS rows

P on RS rows, K on WS rows

BASIC SEED STITCH panel
(outer and middle sections of picture)
TREE OF LIFE panel (main sections of picture)

MOCK cables

Multiples of 7 sts plus 2

Row 1: (RS) *P3, K4, rep from * to last 2 sts, P2.

Row 2: *K2, P3, K2, rep from * to last 2 sts, K2.

Row 3: *P2, K1, P2, K2, rep from * to last 2 sts, P2.

Row 4: *K2, P1, K2, P2, rep from * to last 2 sts, K2.

Row 5: *P2, K3, P2, rep from * to last 2 sts, P2.

Row 6: *K3, P4, rep from * to last 2 sts, K2.

Row 7: *P2, K5, rep from * to last 2 sts, P2.

Row 8: *K2, P5, rep from * to last 2 sts, K2.

Rep these 8 rows.

DOUBLE DIAMOND panel

Panel of 13 sts on St st background

Row 1: (RS) K6, P1, K6.

Row 2: P6, K1, P6.

Row 3: K5, P1, K1, P1, K5.

Row 4: P5, K1, P1, K1, P5.

Row 5: K4, P1, (K1, P1) twice, K4.

Row 6: P4, K1, (P1, K1) twice, P4.

Row 7: K3, P1, (K1, P1) 3 times, K3.

Row 8: P3, K1, (P1, K1) 3 times, P3.

Row 9: K2, P1, K1, P1, K3, P1, K1, P1, K2.

Row 10: P2, K1, P1, K1, P3, K1, P1, K1, P2.

Row 11: (K1, P1) twice, K5, (P1, K1) twice.

Row 12: (P1, K1) twice, P5, (K1, P1) twice.

Row 13: As row 9.

Row 14: As row 10.

Row 15: As row 7.

Row 16: As row 8.

Row 17: As row 5.

Row 18: As row 6.

Row 19: As row 3.

Row 20: As row 4.

Rep these 20 rows.

RIDGE AND FURROW panel

Multiples of 15 sts

Row 1: (RS) K5, (P1, K1) twice, P1, K5.

Row 2: P4, (K1, P2) twice, K1, P4.

Row 3: K3, (P1, K3) 3 times.

Row 4: P2, (K1, P4) twice, K1, P2.

Row 5: K1, (P1, K5) twice, P1, K1.

Row 6: (K1, P6) twice, K1.

Rep these 6 rows.

LADDER panel

Panel of 11 sts on St st background

Rows 1 and 3: (RS) K1, P1, K7, P1, K1.
Row 2: P1, K1, P7, K1, P1.
Row 4: P1, K9, P1.
Rep these 4 rows.

STEPS panel

Panel of 5 sts on St st background

Row 1: (RS) P.
Row 2: (K1, P1) twice, K1.
Rep these 2 rows.

ANCHOR motif

Panel of 11 sts on St st background

Row 1: (RS) K5, P1, K5.
Row 2: P4, K1, P1, K1, P4.
Row 3: K3, (P1, K1) twice, P1, K3.
Row 4: P2, K1, P5, K1, P2.
Row 5: K1, (P1, K3) twice, P1, K1.
Row 6: K1, P9, K1.
Row 7: (P1, K4) twice, P1.
Row 8: P.
Row 9: K5, P1, K5.
Row 10: P.
Row 11: K3, P5, K3.
Row 12: P3, K5, P3.
Row 13: K.
Row 14: P5, K1, P5.
Row 15: K.
Row 16: As row 14.
Row 17: K4, P1, K1, P1, K4.
Row 18: (P3, K1) twice, P3.
Row 19: As row 17.
Row 20: As row 14.
Row 21: K.
Row 22: P.
Rep these 22 rows.

LADDER panel (outer sections of picture)
STEPS panel (inner sections of picture)
ANCHOR motif (central section of picture)

MARRIAGE LINES panel

Panel of 13 sts on St st background

Row 1: (RS) (P1, K1) twice, P1, K7, P1.
Row 2: K1, P6, K1, P1, K1, P2, K1.
Row 3: P1, K3, P1, K1, P1, K5, P1.
Row 4: K1, P4, K1, P1, K1, P4, K1.
Row 5: P1, K5, P1, K1, P1, K3, P1.
Row 6: K1, P2, K1, P1, K1, P6, K1.
Row 7: P1, K7, (P1, K1) twice, P1.
Row 8: As row 6.
Row 9: As row 5.
Row 10: As row 4.
Row 11: As row 3.
Row 12: As row 2.
Rep these 12 rows.

HEART AND STAR motifs

Panel of 19 sts on St st background

Row 1: (RS) K9, P1, K9.
Row 2: P.
Row 3: K3, (P1, K5) twice, P1, K3.
Row 4: P4, K1, P3, K1, P1, K1, P3, K1, P4.
Row 5: K5, (P1, K1) 4 times, P1, K5.
Row 6: P6, (K1, P1) 3 times, K1, P6.
Row 7: As row 5.
Row 8: P4, (K1, P1) 5 times, K1, P4.
Row 9: (K1, P1) 9 times, K1.
Row 10: As row 8.
Row 11: As row 7.
Row 12: As row 6.
Row 13: As row 5.
Row 14: As row 4.
Row 15: As row 3.
Row 16: As row 2.
Row 17: As row 1.
Rows 18 and 20: P.
Row 19: K.
Row 21: As row 1.
Row 22: P8, K3, P8.
Row 23: K7, P2, K1, P2, K7.
Row 24: P6, K2, P3, K2, P6.
Row 25: (K5, P2) twice, K5.
Row 26: P4, K2, P7, K2, P4.
Row 27: K4, P2, K3, P1, K3, P2, K4.
Row 28: P4, K2, P2, K3, P2, K2, P4.
Row 29: K5, P4, K1, P4, K5.
Row 30: As row 24.
Rep these 30 rows.

LIGHTNING panel

Panel of 11 sts on St st background

Row 1: (RS) P1, K1, P1, K7, P1.
Row 2: K1, P6, K1, P2, K1.
Row 3: P1, K3, P1, K5, P1.
Row 4: K1, P4, K1, P4, K1.
Row 5: P1, K5, P1, K3, P1.
Row 6: K1, P2, K1, P6, K1.
Row 7: P1, K7, P1, K1, P1.
Row 8: As row 6.
Row 9: As row 5.
Row 10: As row 4.
Row 11: As row 3.
Row 12: As row 2.
Rep these 12 rows.

MARRIAGE LINES panel (left section of picture)
HEART AND STAR motifs (middle section of picture)
LIGHTNING panel (right section of picture)

68 knit and purl panels

OPEN DIAMOND panel

Panel of 9 sts on St st background

Row 1: (RS) P1, K7, P1.
Row 2: P1, K1, P5, K1, P1.
Row 3: K2, P1, K3, P1, K2.
Row 4: P3, K1, P1, K1, P3.
Row 5: K4, P1, K4.
Row 6: As row 4.
Row 7: As row 3.
Row 8: As row 2.
Rep these 8 rows.

ROUGH MARRIAGE LINES panel

Panel of 10 sts on Reverse St st background

Row 1: (RS) P7, K2, *P8, K2, rep from * to last st, P1.
Row 2: *P1, K1, P2, K6, rep from * to end.
Row 3: *P5, K2, P1, K2, rep from * to end.
Row 4: *P3, K1, P2, K4, rep from * to end.
Row 5: *P3, K2, P1, K4, rep from * to end.
Row 6: *P5, K1, P2, K2, rep from * to end.
Row 7: *P1, K2, P1, K6, rep from * to end.
Row 8: As row 6.
Row 9: As row 5.
Row 10: As row 4.
Row 11: As row 3.
Row 12: As row 2.
Row 13: As row 1.
Row 14: *P2, K8, rep from * to end.
Rep these 14 rows.

SEEDED FLAGS panel

Panel of 9 sts on St st background

Row 1: (RS) K3, P1, K1, P1, K3.
Row 2: P2, K1, P3, K1, P2.
Row 3: (K1, P1) 4 times, K1.
Row 4: (K1, P1) twice, P1, (P1, K1) twice.
Row 5: As row 3.
Row 6: As row 2.
Rep these 6 rows.

OPEN DIAMOND panel (outer and middle sections of picture)
ROUGH MARRIAGE LINES panel (left inner section of picture)
SEEDED FLAGS panel (right inner section of picture)

70 knit and purl panels

FLAGS AND STRIPES panel

Panel of 8 sts on St st background

Row 1: (RS) P.
Row 2: K.
Row 3: K5, P2, K1.
Row 4: P2, K2, P4.
Row 5: K3, P2, K3.
Row 6: P4, K2, P2.
Row 7: K1, P2, K5.
Row 8: P5, K2, P1.
Row 9: K2, P2, K4.
Row 10: P3, K2, P3.
Row 11: K4, P2, K2.
Row 12: P1, K2, P5.
Rep these 12 rows.

SIMPLE STAR motif

Panel of 19 sts on St st background

Row 1: (WS) P.
Row 2: K.
Row 3: P9, K1, P9.
Row 4: K8, P1, K1, P1, K8.
Row 5: P1, K1, (P7, K1) twice, P1.
Row 6: K2, P1, K5, P1, K1, P1, K5, P1, K2.
Row 7: (P1, K1) twice, P5, K1, P5, (K1, P1) twice.
Row 8: K2, (P1, K1, P1, K3) twice, P1, K1, P1, K2.
Row 9: P3, K1, P1, (K1, P3) twice, K1, P1, K1, P3.
Row 10: K4, (P1, K1) 5 times, P1, K4.
Row 11: P5, (K1, P1) 4 times, K1, P5.
Row 12: K6, P1, K5, P1, K6.
Row 13: (P1, K1) 3 times, P2, K1, P1, K1, P2, (K1, P1) 3 times.
Row 14: (P1, K1) 3 times, P1, (K2, P1) twice, (K1, P1) 3 times.
Row 15: As row 13.
Row 16: As row 12.
Row 17: As row 11.
Row 18: As row 10.
Row 19: As row 9.
Row 20: As row 8.
Row 21: As row 7.
Row 22: As row 6.
Row 23: As row 5.
Row 24: As row 4.
Row 25: As row 3.
Row 26: As row 2.
Rep these 26 rows.

BROKEN CHEVRON panel

Panel of 18 sts on Reverse St st background

Row 1: (RS) (K1, P2, K2, P2, K1, P1) twice.
Row 2: K3, P2, K2, P2, K1, (P2, K2) twice.
Row 3: P1, K2, P2, K2, P3, (K2, P2) twice.
Row 4: K1, P2, K2, P2, K5, P2, K2, P2.
Rep these 4 rows.

MOSS ZIGZAG panel

Panel of 14 sts on St st background

Row 1: (RS) (P1, K1, P1, K4) twice.
Row 2: (P4, K1, P1, K1) twice.
Row 3: ((K1, P1) twice, K3) twice.
Row 4: (P3, (K1, P1) twice) twice.
Row 5: K2, (P1, K1) twice, K3, (P1, K1) twice, K1.
Row 6: P2, (K1, P1) twice, P3, (K1, P1) twice, P1.
Row 7: (K3, (P1, K1) twice) twice.
Row 8: ((P1, K1) twice, P3) twice.
Row 9: K4, (P1, K1) twice, K3, P1, K1, P1.
Row 10: ((K1, P1) twice, P3) twice.
Row 11: As row 7.
Row 12: As row 8.
Row 13: As row 5.
Row 14: As row 6.
Row 15: As row 3.
Row 16: As row 4.
Rep these 16 rows.

STOCKINETTE STITCH FLAGS panel

Panel of 13 sts on Reverse St st background

Row 1: (RS) K4, P1, K3, P1, K4.
Row 2: (P3, K2) twice, P3.
Row 3: K2, P3, K3, P3, K2.
Row 4: P1, K4, P3, K4, P1.
Row 5: P5, K3, P5.
Row 6: As row 4.
Row 7: As row 3.
Row 8: As row 2.
Rep these 8 rows.

DOUBLE HERRINGBONE panel

Panel of 17 sts on St st background

Row 1: (RS) (P1, K7) twice, P1.
Row 2: K1, P6, K1, P1, K1, P6, K1.
Row 3: P1, K5, (P1, K1) twice, P1, K5, P1.
Row 4: K1, P4, (K1, P1) 3 times, K1, P4, K1.
Row 5: P1, K3, (P1, K1) twice, K1, (K1, P1) twice, K3, P1.
Row 6: K1, P2, (K1, P1) twice, P3, (K1, P1) twice, P2, K1.
Row 7: (P1, K1) 3 times, K5, (K1, P1) 3 times.
Row 8: K2, P1, K1, P9, K1, P1, K2.
Row 9: (P1, K1) twice, K9, (K1, P1) twice.
Row 10: K2, P13, K2.
Row 11: P1, K15, P1.
Row 12: K1, P15, P1.
Rep these 12 rows.

Ribs

Vertical lines on a relatively small scale characterize ribs, and this section presents a wide selection. To be truly practical for traditional welts, cuffs, and necklines, ribs should stretch, contract, and provide a firm, durable edging to the main fabric. However, some ribs perform these tasks more effectively than others. The basic Knit One, Purl One and Knit Two, Purl Two ribs function the best of all. In contrast, for example, Blanket rib is not very elastic, and Raised Eyelet rib is not firm enough to do the same job. However, all have a place, and many fashionable garments look stunning with purely decorative welts or when ribs provide an overall pattern.

Use needles one or two sizes smaller than those for the main fabric if you want to keep a welt firm and select a woolen yarn rather than a cotton for more elasticity.

KNIT ONE, PURL ONE rib (reversible)
Odd number of sts
Row 1: *K1, P1, rep from * to last st, K1.
Row 2: *P1, K1, rep from * to last st, P1.
Rep these 2 rows.

KNIT TWO, PURL TWO rib (reversible)
Multiples of 4 sts plus 2
Row 1: *K2, P2, rep from * to last 2 sts, K2.
Row 2: *P2, K2, rep from * to last 2 sts, P2.
Rep these 2 rows.

SEEDED rib (reversible)
Multiples of 4 sts plus 3
Row 1: K3, *P1, K3, rep from * to end.
Row 2: K1, *P1, K3, rep from * to last 2 sts, P1, K1.
Rep these 2 rows.

KNIT ONE, PURL ONE rib (top section of picture)
KNIT TWO, PURL TWO rib (middle section of picture)
SEEDED rib (bottom section of picture)

CABLE AND EYELET rib

Multiples of 10 sts plus 4

Row 1: (RS) P1, K2 tog, yfrn, *P2, K4, P2, K2tog, yfrn, rep from * to last st, P1.

Row 2 and all WS rows: K1, P2, *K2, P4, K2, P2, rep from * to last st, K1.

Row 3: P1, yon, SKP, *P2, C4F, P2, yrn, SKP, rep from * to last st, P1.

Row 5: As row 1.

Row 7: P1, yon, SKP, *P2, K4, P2, yrn, SKP, rep from * to last st, P1.

Row 8: As row 2.

Rep these 8 rows.

SPIRAL rib

Multiples of 9 sts plus 3

Row 1: (RS) *P3, C2B 3 times, rep from * to last 3 sts, P3.

Row 2: *K3, P6, rep from * to last 3 sts, K3.

Row 3: *P3, K1, C2B twice, K1, rep from * to last 3 sts, P3.

Row 4: *K3, P6, rep from * to last 3 sts, K3.

Rep these 4 rows.

DIAGONAL rib

Multiples of 4 sts

Row 1: (RS) *K2, P2, rep from * to end.

Row 2: As row 1.

Row 3: *K1, P2, K1, rep from * to end.

Row 4: *P1, K2, P1, rep from * to end.

Row 5: *P2, K2, rep from * to end.

Row 6: As row 5.

Row 7: *P1, K2, P1, rep from * to end.

Row 8: *K1, P2, K1, rep from * to end.

Rep these 8 rows.

TIP Diagonal patterns tend to stretch on the bias. To minimize this, choose firmly twisted yarns, not soft ones, and don't wring the fabric when washing it.

CABLE AND EYELET rib (top section of picture)
SPIRAL rib (middle section of picture)
DIAGONAL rib (bottom section of picture)

CORDED rib

Multiples of 6 sts

Cr2F = K 2nd st on LHN tfl, then K first st and slip both off LHN

Row 1: (RS) *P2, Cr2F, K2, rep from * to end.

Rows 2 and all WS rows: *P4, K2, rep from * to end.

Row 3: *P2, K1, Cr2F, K1, rep from * to end.

Row 5: *P2, K2, Cr2F, rep from * to end.

Row 6: As row 2.

Rep these 6 rows.

RICKRACK rib

Multiples of 5 sts plus 1

Cr2F = K 2nd st on LHN tfl, then K first st and slip both off LHN

Cr2PB = P 2nd st on LHN tbl, then P first st and slip both off LHN

Row 1: (RS) K1, *P1, Cr2F, P1, K1, rep from * to end.

Row 2: *P1, K1, Cr2PB, K1, rep from * to last st, P1.

Rep these 2 rows.

TWISTED rib

Multiples of 4 sts plus 2

Cr2F = K 2nd st on LHN tfl, then K first st and slip both off LHN

Rows 1 and 3: (RS) P2, *K2, P2, rep from * to end.

Row 2 and all WS rows: K2, *P2, K2, rep from * to end.

Row 5: P2, *Cr2F, P2, rep from * to end.

Row 6: As row 2.

Rep these 6 rows.

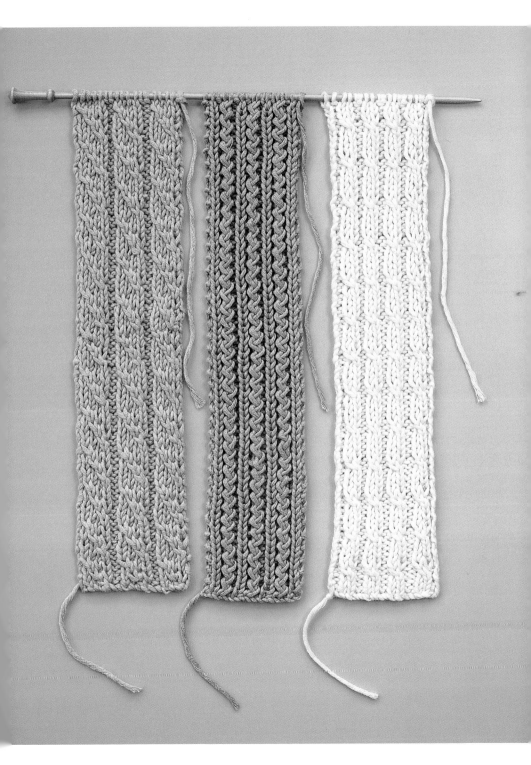

MOCK CABLE rib

Multiples of 5 sts plus 2

Row 1: (RS) *P2, K3, rep from * to last 2 sts, P2.

Row 2: K2, *P3, K2, rep from * to end.

Row 3: *P2, sl1, K2, yfrn, psso the K2 and yfrn, rep from * to last 2 sts, P2.

Row 4: As row 2.

Rep these 4 rows.

CROSSED rib

Multiples of 4 sts plus 1

Cr3B = slip 2 sts onto CN and hold at back of work, K1, slip P st onto LHN and P it, K1 from CN

Row 1: (RS) *P1, K1, rep from * to last st, P1.

Row 2 and all WS rows: K1, *P1, K1, rep from * to end.

Row 3: As row 1.

Row 5: *P1, Cr3B, rep from * to last st, P1.

Row 6: As row 2.

Rep these 6 rows.

OPEN TWISTED rib

Multiples of 5 sts plus 3

Row 1: (RS) *P1, K1 tbl, P1, K2, rep from * to last 3 sts, P1, K1 tbl, P1.

Row 2: K1, P1 tbl, K1, *P2, K1, P1 tbl, K1, rep from * to end.

Row 3: *P1, K1 tbl, P1, K1, yfwd, K1, rep from * to last 3 sts, P1, K1 tbl, P1.

Row 4: K1, P1 tbl, K1, * P3, K1, P1 tbl, K1, rep from * to end.

Row 5: *P1, K1 tbl, P1, K3, pass 3rd st on RHN over first 2 sts, rep from * to last 3 sts, P1, K1 tbl, P1.

Rep rows 2–5.

MOCK CABLE rib (top section of picture)
CROSSED rib (middle section of picture)
OPEN TWISTED rib (bottom section of picture)

WOVEN rib

Multiples of 2 sts plus 1
Row 1: (RS) *K1, yfwd, sl1, ybk,
rep from * to last st, K1.
Row 2: P.
Rep these 2 rows.

SUPPLE rib

Multiples of 3 sts plus 1
Row 1: (RS) *K1, K1 but leave
on LHN, yfwd, P1 into same and
next st tog, ybk, rep from * to
last st, K1.
Row 2: P.
Rep these 2 rows.

LACY rib

Multiples of 5 sts plus 2
Row 1: (RS) P2, *K1, yfwd, SKP,
P2, rep from * to end.
Row 2: K2, *P3, K2, rep from *
to end.
Row 3: P2, *K2tog, yfwd, K1, P2,
rep from * to end.
Row 4: As row 2.
Rep these 4 rows.

WOVEN rib (left section of picture)
SUPPLE rib (middle section of picture)
LACY rib (right section of picture)

OPENWORK rib

Multiples of 4 sts plus 2

Rows 1, 3, and 5: (WS) *K2, P2, rep from * to last 2 sts, K2.

Rows 2 and 4: P2, *K2, P2, rep from * to end.

Row 6: P2, *yrn, SKP, P2, rep from * to end.

Rep these 6 rows.

RAISED EYELET rib

Multiples of 7 sts plus 2

Row 1: (RS) *P2, K2tog, yfwd, K1, yfwd, SKP, rep from * to last 2 sts, P2.

Row 2: K2, *P5, K2, rep from * to end.

Row 3: *P2, K5, rep from * to last 2 sts, P2.

Row 4: As row 2.

Rep these 4 rows.

BLANKET rib

Multiples of 2 sts plus 1

Row 1: (RS) inc1 K in each st.

Row 2: K2tog, *P2tog, K2tog, rep from * to end.

Rep these 2 rows.

OPENWORK rib (top section of picture)
RAISED EYELET rib (middle section of picture)
BLANKET rib (bottom section of picture)

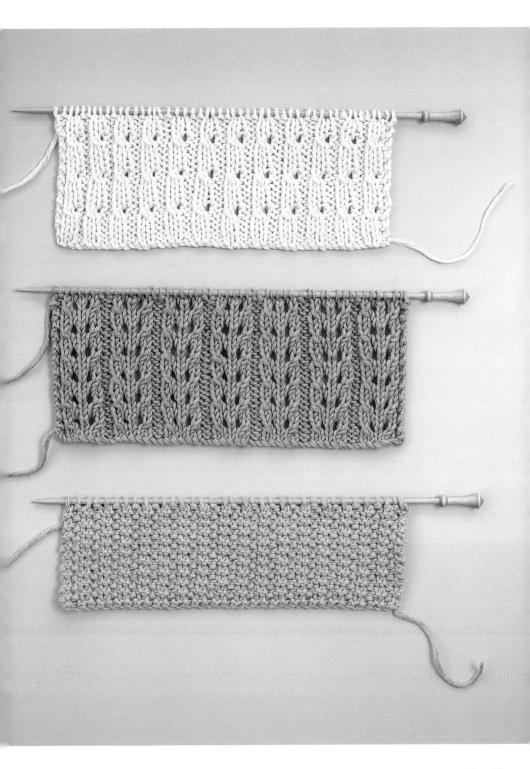

DOUBLE RICKRACK rib

Multiples of 7 sts plus 3

Cr2B = K 2nd st on LHN tbl, then K first st and slip both off LHN

Cr2F = K 2nd st on LHN tfl, then K first st and slip both off LHN

Row 1: (RS) *P3, Cr2B, Cr2F, rep from * to last 3 sts, P3.

Row 2: K3, *P4, K3, rep from * to end.

Row 3: *P3, Cr2F, Cr2B, rep from * to last 3 sts, P3.

Row 4: K3, *P4, K3, rep from * to end.

Rep these 4 rows.

ALTERNATING CABLE rib

Multiples of 9 sts plus 3

Row 1: (RS) *P3, K6, rep from * to last 3 sts, P3.

Row 2 and all WS rows: *K3, P6, rep from * to last 3 sts, K3.

Row 3: *P3, C4B, K2, rep from * to last 3 sts, P3.

Row 5: *P3, K2, C4F, rep from * to last 3 sts, P3.

Row 6: As row 2.

Rep rows 3–6.

FEATHER rib

Multiples of 5 sts plus 2

Row 1: (RS) P2, *yfrn, K2tog tbl, K1, P2, rep from * to end.

Row 2: K2, *yfwd, K2tog tbl, P1 tbl, K2, rep from * to end.

Rep these 2 rows.

DOUBLE RICKRACK rib (top section of picture)
ALTERNATING CABLE rib (middle section of picture)
FEATHER rib (bottom section of picture)

Textured stitches

This section draws together stitch patterns that create a textured fabric—some of them subtly and others more flamboyantly. They also have a mixed heritage. Trinity stitch is often associated with Aran designs and has distinctly religious connotations with its three-in-one and one-in-three construction. The name Linen stitch clearly reflects the fabric it creates, and Gathered stitch delivers just what it promises.

As such, the stitch patterns here represent a real exploration of various techniques to create different textures. Twisting knit stitches across a purl background takes them in a winding path to the left or right. Crossing two knit stitches produces a miniature cable, which can be worked either with or without a cable needle according to preference. Both of these techniques reduce the elasticity of the fabric, as with Double Trellis pattern. Very firm fabrics evolve from stitches such as Risotto and Spine stitch. Other techniques include matching increases and decreases to make textures such as Trinity stitch and wrapping the yarn around stitches to cluster them or around the needle to elongate them. Happy exploring!

LONG BOBBLE stitch
Multiples of 6 sts plus 3
Row 1: (WS) P to end.
Row 2: K1, *K3, (K1, yfwd, K1) into next st, K1, (turn, P5, turn, K5) twice, K1, rep from * to last 2 sts, K2.
Row 3: P1, *P2, P2tog, P1, P2tog tbl, P1, rep from * to last 2 sts, P2.
Row 4: K3, *K4, (K1, yfwd, K1) into next st, K1, (turn, P5, turn, K5) twice, rep from * to last 6 sts, K6.
Row 5: P3, *P3, P2tog, P1, P2tog tbl, rep from * to last 6 sts, P6.
Rep rows 2–5.

TRELLIS pattern
Multiples of 8 sts plus 2
Cr2B = K 2nd st on LHN tbl, then K first st and slip both off LHN
Cr2F = K 2nd st on LHN tfl, then K first st and slip both off LHN
Row 1: (WS) P4, K2, *P6, K2, rep from * to last 4 sts, P4.
Row 2: K2, *Cr2B, P2, Cr2F, K2, rep from * to end.
Row 3: P3, K4, *P4, K4, rep from * to last 3 sts, P3.
Row 4: K1, *Cr2B, P4, Cr2F, rep from * to last st, K1.
Row 5: K2, *P6, K2, rep from * to end.
Row 6: P2, *Cr2F, K2, Cr2B, P2, rep from * to end.
Row 7: K3, P4, *K4, P4, rep from * to last 3 sts, K3.
Row 8: P3, Cr2F, Cr2B, *P4, Cr2F, Cr2B, rep from * to last 3 sts, P3.
Rep these 8 rows.

GOOSEBERRY stitch
Multiples of 2 sts plus 1
Row 1: (RS) K.
Row 2: K1, *(P1, yrn, P1, yrn, P1) into next st, K1, rep from * to end.
Row 3: P.
Row 4: K1, *yfwd, sl2, P3tog, p2sso, ybk, K1, rep from * to end.
Row 5: K.
Row 6: K1, *K1, (P1, yrn, P1, yrn, P1) into next st, rep from * to last 2 sts, K2.
Row 7: P.
Row 8: K1, *K1, yfwd, sl2, P3tog, p2sso, ybk, rep from * to last 2 sts, K2.
Rep these 8 rows.

LONG BOBBLE stitch (top section of picture)
TRELLIS pattern (middle section of picture)
GOOSEBERRY stitch (bottom section of picture)

SLIPPED GRANITE stitch

Multiples of 4 sts plus 2

Row 1: (WS) *K1, P1, rep from * to end.

Row 2: *P1, ybk, sl1, K2, yfrn, psso the K2 and yfrn, rep from * to last 2 sts, P1, K1.

Row 3: As row 1.

Row 4: P1, K1, *P1, ybk, sl1, K2, yfrn, psso the K2 and yfrn, rep from * to end.

Rep these 4 rows.

LINEN stitch

Multiples of 2 sts

Row 1: (RS) *K1, yfwd, sl1, ybk, rep from * to end.

Row 2: *P1, ybk, sl1, yfwd, rep from * to end.

Rep these 2 rows.

TRINITY stitch

Multiples of 4 sts plus 2

Row 1: (RS) P.

Row 2: K1, *(K1, P1, K1) into next st, P3tog, rep from * to last st, K1.

Row 3: P.

Row 4: K1, *P3tog, (K1, P1, K1) into next st, rep from * to last st, K1.

Rep these 4 rows.

SLIPPED GRANITE stitch (top section of picture)

LINEN stitch (middle section of picture)

TRINITY stitch (bottom section of picture)

WOVEN brocade

Multiples of 10 sts plus 2

Row 1: (RS) K1, *K1, yfwd, sl3, ybk, K2, yfwd, sl3, ybk, K1, rep from * to last st, K1.

Row 2: sl1, *ybk, sl3, yfwd, P2, rep from * to last st, sl1.

Row 3: K1, yfwd, sl1, *ybk, K2, yfwd, sl3, rep from * to last 5 sts, ybk, K2, yfwd, sl2, ybk, K1.

Row 4: sl1, ybk, sl1, yfwd, *P2, ybk, sl3, yfwd, rep from * to last 5 sts, P2, ybk, sl2, yfwd, sl1.

Row 5: K1, *yfwd, sl3, ybk, K2, rep from * to last st, K1.

Row 6: sl1, *P1, ybk, sl3, yfwd, P1, rep from * to last st, sl1.

Row 7: As row 5.

Row 8: As row 4.

Row 9: As row 3.

Row 10: As row 2.

Rep these 10 rows.

BLACKBERRY stitch

Multiples of 4 sts

Row 1: (RS) *(K1, yfwd, K1) into next st, P3, rep from * to end.

Row 2: *P3tog, K3, rep from * to end.

Row 3: *P3, (K1, yfwd, K1) into next st, rep from * to end.

Row 4: *K3, P3tog, rep from * to end.

Rep these 4 rows.

SPINE stitch

Multiples of 4 sts

Cr2B = K 2nd st on LHN tbl, then K first st and slip both off LHN

Cr2F = K 2nd st on LHN tfl, then K first st and slip both off LHN

Row 1: (RS) *Cr2B, Cr2F, rep from * to end.

Row 2: P.

Rep these 2 rows.

WOVEN brocade (top section of picture)
BLACKBERRY stitch (middle section of picture)
SPINE stitch (bottom section of picture)

PLAITED BASKET stitch

Multiples of 2 sts

Cr2B = K 2nd st on LHN tbl, then K first st and slip both off LHN

Cr2F = P 2nd st on LHN tfl, then P first st tfl and slip both off LHN

Row 1: (RS) *Cr2B, rep from * to end.

Row 2: P1, * Cr2F, rep from * to last st, P1.

Rep these 2 rows.

TRELLIS stitch

Multiples of 6 sts

T3L = slip 1 st onto CN and hold at front of work, P2, K1 from CN

T3R = slip 2 sts onto CN and hold at back of work, K1, P2 from CN

Rows 1 and 3: (RS) *P2, K2, P2, rep from * to end.

Rows 2 and 4: *K2, P2, K2, rep from * to end.

Row 5: *T3R, T3L, rep from * to end.

Rows 6, 8, and 10: *P1, K4, P1, rep from * to end.

Rows 7 and 9: *K1, P4, K1, rep from * to end.

Row 11: *T3L, T3R, rep from * to end.

Row12: As row 2.

Rep these 12 rows.

PEBBLE stitch

Multiples of 2 sts

Row 1: (RS) K.

Row 2: P.

Row 3: K1, *K2tog, rep from * to last st, K1.

Row 4: K1, *K1 in horizontal bar before next st, K1, rep from * to last st, K1.

Rep these 4 rows.

PLAITED BASKET stitch (top section of picture)
TRELLIS stitch (middle section of picture)
PEBBLE stitch (bottom section of picture)

RIDGED SLIP stitch

Multiples of 4 sts
Row 1: (RS) *K3, sl1, rep from * to end.
Row 2: ybk, *sl1, yfwd, P3, rep from * to end.
Row 3: As row 1.
Row 4: K.
Row 5: *K1, sl1, ybk, K2, rep from * to end.
Row 6: *P2, sl1, yfwd, P1, rep from * to end.
Row 7: As row 5.
Row 8: K.
Rep these 8 rows.

TUCKED STOCKINETTE stitch

Multiples of any number
Rows 1, 3, and 5: (RS) K.
Rows 2, 4, 6, and 7: P.
Rows 8, 10, and 12: P.
Rows 9 and 11: K.
Row 13: *Fold at ridge, pick up first st of row 2 from back, K tog with first st on LHN tbl, rep from * to end.
Rows 14, 16, and 18: P.
Rows 15, 17, and 19: K.
Rep rows 2–19.

GATHERED stitch

Multiples of any number
Rows 1–6: K.
Row 7: (RS) inc1 K in each st.
Rows 8, 10, and 12: P.
Rows 9 and 11: K.
Row 13: *K2tog, rep from * to end.
Rep rows 2–13.

RIDGED SLIP stitch (top section of picture)
TUCKED STOCKINETTE stitch (middle section of picture)
GATHERED stitch (bottom section of picture)

98 textured stitches

RISOTTO stitch (reversible)

Multiples of 2 sts

Rows 1 and 3: (RS) K.

Row 2: *P2tog but leave the 2 sts on LHN, ybk, K tog same 2 sts, rep from * to end.

Row 4: P1, *P2tog but leave the 2 sts on LHN, ybk, K tog same 2 sts, rep from * to last st, P1.

Row 5: K.

Rep rows 2–5.

WAFFLE stitch

Multiples of 2 sts

Row 1: (RS) K.

Row 2: K.

Row 3: *K1, K1 through center of st in row below, rep from * to end.

Row 4: *K tog next st and longer loop at its base, K1, rep from * to end.

Row 5: *K1 through center of st in row below, K1, rep from * to end.

Row 6: *K1, K tog next st and longer loop at its base, rep from * to end.

Rep rows 3–6.

CLAM stitch

Multiples of 6 sts plus 1

Row 1: (RS) K.

Row 2: P1, *(yrn, P1) 5 times, P1, rep from * to end.

Row 3: *K1, sl5 to RHN dropping extra loops, pass 5 sts back to LHN, (yfrn, K1, (yfrn, P1, yon, K1) twice) into same 5 sts tog, rep from * to last st, K1.

Row 4: *P1, K5 dropping extra loops, rep from * to last st, P1.

Row 5: K.

Row 6: *P4, (yrn, P1) 5 times, P1, rep from * to last 3 sts, P3.

Row 7: K3, *K1, work next 5 sts as in row 3, rep from * to last 4 sts, K4.

Row 8: P4, *K5 dropping extra loops, P1, rep from * to last 3 sts, P3.

Rep these 8 rows.

RISOTTO stitch (top section of picture)
WAFFLE stitch (middle section of picture)
CLAM stitch (bottom section of picture)

OVERLAPPING LEAVES pattern

Multiples of 24 sts plus 1

Row 1: (RS) K1, *M1, SKP, K4, K2tog, K3, M1, K1, M1, K3, SKP, K4, K2tog, M1, K1, rep from * to end.

Row 2 and all WS rows: P.

Row 3: K1, *M1, K1, SKP, K2, K2tog, K4, M1, K1, M1, K4, SKP, K2, K2tog, K1, M1, K1, rep from * to end.

Row 5: K1, *M1, K2, SKP, K2tog, K5, M1, K1, M1, K5, SKP, K2tog, K2, M1, K1, rep from * to end.

Row 7: K1, *M1, K3, SKP, K4, K2tog, M1, K1, M1, SKP, K4, K2tog, K3, M1, K1, rep from * to end.

Row 9: K1, *M1, K4, SKP, K2, K2tog, (K1, M1) twice, K1, SKP, K2, K2tog, K4, M1, K1, rep from * to end.

Row 11: K1, *M1, K5, SKP, K2tog, K2, M1, K1, M1, K2, SKP, K2tog, K5, M1, K1, rep from * to end.

Row 12: P.

Rep these 12 rows.

BAMBOO stitch

Multiples of 2 sts

Row 1: (RS) K1, *yrn, K2, pass previous yrn over K2, rep from * to last st, K1.

Row 2: P.

Rep these 2 rows.

WOVEN LADDER stitch

Multiples of 8 sts plus 1

Row 1: (RS) *K5, yfwd, sl3, ybk, rep from * to last st, K1.

Row 2: P1, *ybk, sl3, yfwd, P5, rep from * to end.

Row 3: As row 1.

Row 4: P.

Row 5: K1, *yfwd, sl3, ybk, K5, rep from * to end.

Row 6: P1, *P4, ybk, sl3, yfwd, P1, rep from * to end.

Row 7: As row 5.

Row 8: As row 4.

Rep these 8 rows.

OVERLAPPING LEAVES pattern (top section of picture)
BAMBOO stitch (middle section of picture)
WOVEN LADDER stitch (bottom section of picture)

RIPPLE stitch

Multiples of 3 sts
Row 1: (RS) *K2tog but leave on LHN, K first st again and slip both off LHN, K1, rep from * to end.
Row 2: P.
Row 3: *K1, K2tog, K into first st again as row 1, rep from * to end.
Row 4: P.
Rep these 4 rows.

DOUBLE TRELLIS pattern

Multiples of 6 sts plus 4
RT2L = (raised twist left) K 2nd st tbl, K first and 2nd sts tog tbl
RT2R = (raised twist right) K2tog but leave sts on LHN, K first st again and slip both off LHN
Row 1 and all WS rows: P.
Row 2: *RT2L, RT2R twice, rep from * to last 4 sts, RT2L, RT2R.
Row 4: K1, RT2L, *RT2R, RT2L twice, rep from * to last st, K1.
Row 6: RT2L twice, *K2, RT2L twice, rep from * to end.
Row 8: K1, *RT2L twice, RT2R, rep from * to last 3 sts, RT2L, K1.
Row 10: RT2R, * RT2L, RT2R twice, rep from * to last 2 sts, RT2L.
Row 12: K3, *RT2R twice, K2, rep from * to last st, K1.
Rep these 12 rows.

CROSS stitch

Multiples of 8 sts plus 4
Cr6L = slip 6 sts onto RHN dropping extra loops, slip same 6 sts onto LHN, K 4th, 5th, and 6th sts tbl, K first, 2nd, and 3rd sts, slip all 6 sts off LHN tog
Cr6R = slip 6 sts onto RHN dropping extra loops, slip same 6 sts onto LHN, K 4th, 5th, and 6th sts, K first, 2nd, and 3rd sts, slip all 6 sts off LHN tog
Row 1: (RS) K.
Row 2: K3, * yfrn, P1, (yrn, P1) 5 times, K2, rep from * to last st, K1.
Row 3: K1, *K2, Cr6R, rep from * to last st, K3.
Row 4: K1, P2, K2, * yfrn, P1, (yrn, P1) 5 times, K2, rep from * to last 5 sts, P4, K1.
Row 5: K5, *K2, Cr6L, rep from * to last 5 sts, K7.
Rep rows 2–5.

TIP This stitch is not reversible, but the reverse has an attractive texture.

RIPPLE stitch (top section of picture)
DOUBLE TRELLIS pattern (middle section of picture)
CROSS stitch (bottom section of picture)

DIAMOND TRELLIS pattern

Multiples of 6 sts plus 2

Cr2B = K 2nd st on LHN tbl, then K first st and slip both off LHN

Cr2F = K 2nd st on LHN tfl, then K first st and slip both off LHN

Row 1: (RS) K3, *Cr2B, K4, rep from * to last 5 sts, Cr2B, K3.

Row 2 and all WS rows: P.

Row 3: *K2, Cr2B, Cr2F, rep from * to last 2 sts, K2.

Row 5: K1, *Cr2B, K2, Cr2F, rep from * to last st, K1.

Row 7: *Cr2B, K4, rep from * to last 2 sts, Cr2B.

Row 9: K1, *Cr2F, K2, Cr2B, rep from * to last st, K1.

Row 11: *K2, Cr2F, Cr2B, rep from * to last 2 sts, K2.

Row 12: P.

Rep these 12 rows.

DIAGONAL GRAIN stitch

Multiples of 4 sts plus 1

Rows 1 and 3: (RS) K.

Row 2: P1, *yrn, P2, pass yrn over P2, P2, rep from * to end.

Row 4: P1, *P2, yrn, P2, pass yrn over P2, rep from * to end.

Rep these 4 rows.

INTERLOCKING LEAVES pattern

Multiples of 16 sts plus 1

Cr2B = K 2nd st on LHN tbl, then K first st and slip both off LHN

Cr2F = K 2nd st on LHN tfl, then K first st and slip both off LHN

Row 1: (RS) K1, *K1, Cr2B twice, Cr2F, P1, Cr2B, Cr2F twice, K2, rep from * to end.

Row 2 and all WS rows: P.

Row 3: *K1, Cr2B twice, Cr2F, K1, P1, K1, Cr2B, Cr2F twice, K1, rep from * to end.

Row 5: K1, *K1, Cr2B, Cr2F twice, P1, Cr2B twice, Cr2F, K2, rep from * to end.

Row 7: K1, *Cr2B, Cr2F twice, K1, P1, K1, Cr2B twice, Cr2F, K1, rep from * to end.

Row 9: K1, *K1, Cr2F 3 times, P1, Cr2B 3 times, K2, rep from * to end.

Row 11: K1, *Cr2F 3 times, K1, P1, K1, Cr2B 3 times, K1, rep from * to end.

Row 13: As row 9.

Row 15: As row 7.

Row 17: As row 5.

Row 19: As row 3.

Row 21: As row 1.

Row 23: K1, *Cr2B 3 times, K1, P1, K1, Cr2F 3 times, K1, rep from * to end.

Row 25: K1, *K1, Cr2B 3 times, P1, Cr2F 3 times, K2, rep from * to end.

Row 27: As row 23.

Row 28: P.

Rep these 28 rows.

DIAMOND TRELLIS pattern (top section of picture)
DIAGONAL GRAIN stitch (middle section of picture)
INTERLOCKING LEAVES pattern (bottom section of picture)

ELONGATED stitch
Multiples of 14 sts plus 5
Rows 1 and 3: (RS) K.
Rows 2 and 4: P.
Row 5: K4, *(K1, yfrn) 3 times, (K1, yfrn twice) 4 times, (K1, yfrn) 3 times, K4, rep from * to last st, K1.
Row 6: P, dropping all extra loops.
Rows 7 and 9: K.
Rows 8 and 10: P.
Row 11: K7, *K4, (K1, yfrn) 3 times, (K1, yfrn twice) 4 times, (K1, yfrn) 3 times, rep from * to last st, K12.
Row 12: P, dropping all extra loops.
Rep these 12 rows.

WOVEN BUTTERFLY stitch
Multiples of 10 sts plus 7
make butterfly = slip RHN under 4 long loops, K next st pulling new st under long loops
Rows 1, 3, 5, and 7: (RS) K6, *yfwd, sl5, ybk, K5, rep from * to last st, K1.
Row 2 and all WS rows: P.
Row 9: K8, *make butterfly, K9, rep from * to last 9 sts, make butterfly, K8.
Rows 11, 13, 15, and 17: K1, yfwd, sl5, ybk, *K5, yfwd, sl5, ybk, rep from * to last st, K1.
Row 19: K3, make butterfly, *K9, make butterfly, rep from * to last 3 sts, K3.
Row 20: P.
Rep these 20 rows.

CLUSTER stitch
Multiples of 8 sts plus 5
make cluster = slip next 3 sts onto CN, wrap yarn around sts 6 times counterclockwise, K3 from CN
Row 1: (RS) K.
Row 2 and all WS rows: P.
Row 3: *K5, make cluster, rep from * to last 5 sts, K5.
Row 5: As row 3.
Row 7: *K1, make cluster, K4, rep from * to last 5 sts, K1, make cluster, K1.
Row 8: P.
Rep these 8 rows.

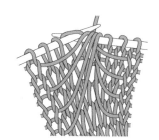

Knit the next stitch, pulling it under the four long loops.

ELONGATED stitch (top section of picture)
WOVEN BUTTERFLY stitch (middle section of picture)
CLUSTER stitch (bottom section of picture)

Edgings

Most stitch patterns need an edging, or ribbing, to stop the knitted fabric from curling or to give extra strength to the finished piece. Some edgings are knitted sideways to produce a band long enough, when slightly stretched, to fit and be sewn around the edge. Others can be knitted as an integral part either before or after knitting the main fabric. The length of the knitted-on variety depends on the gauge and the number of stitches, so it's wise to knit a gauge swatch.

This selection of edgings ranges from the very simple finishes shown opposite to the more dramatic Double Frill, Ruffled, and Knotted edgings. It includes some very pretty open edgings. All of these can be worked in medium-weight yarns for a substantial feel, and some of them look exquisite knitted in very fine Shetland wool to give the gossamer quality of Shetland lace. The photographs will give you some inspiration, but experiment for different effects.

STOCKINETTE STITCH edging
Cast on sts for finished number required
Rows 1, 3, and 5: (RS) K.
Rows 2, 4, and 6: P.

PURL RIDGE hem
Cast on sts for finished number required
Rows 1, 3, 5, and 7: (RS) K.
Rows 2, 4, 6, and 8: P.
Row 9: P.
Rows 10, 12, 14, 16, and 18: P.
Rows 11, 13, 15, and 17: K.
Fold under along the purl ridge and slip stitch edging in place.

PICOT RIDGE hem
Multiples of 2 sts plus 1
Rows 1 and 3: (RS) K.
Row 2 and all WS rows: P.
Row 5: K1, *yfwd, K2tog, rep from * to end.
Rows 7, 8, and 9: K.
Fold under along the picot row and slip stitch edging in place.

STOCKINETTE STITCH edging (top section of picture)
PURL RIDGE hem (middle section of picture)
PICOT RIDGE hem (bottom section of picture)

SIMPLE LOOP edging

Multiples of 6 sts plus 3 (top edge decreases to half as many sts)

Row 1: (RS) K3, *bind off 3 sts, K3, rep from * to end.
Rows 2–5: K.

TREE OF LIFE edging

Multiples of 13 sts

Row 1: (RS) *K1, yfwd, K4, SK2P, K4, yfwd, K1, rep from * to end.
Row 2: *P2, K9, P2, rep from * to end.
Row 3: *K2, yfwd, K3, SK2P, K3, yfwd, K2, rep from * to end.
Row 4: *P3, K7, P3, rep from * to end.
Row 5: *K3, yfwd, K2, SK2P, K2, yfwd, K3, rep from * to end.
Row 6: *P4, K5, P4, rep from * to end.
Row 7: *K4, yfwd, K1, SK2P, K1, yfwd, K4, rep from * to end.
Row 8: *P5, K3, P5, rep from * to end.
Row 9: *K5, yfwd, SK2P, yfwd, K5, rep from * to end.
Row 10: P.

WAVE edging

Multiples of 18 sts plus 2

Row 1: (RS) K.
Row 2: P.
Row 3: K1, *K2tog 3 times, (yfwd, K1) 6 times, K2tog 3 times, rep from * to last st, K1.
Row 4: K.
Rows 5–12: Rep rows 1–4 twice.

SIMPLE LOOP edging (top section of picture)
TREE OF LIFE edging (middle section of picture)
WAVE edging (bottom section of picture)

GARTER STITCH frill

Cast on half as many sts as finished number required

Rows 1–3: K.

Rows 4, 6, 8, and 10: (RS) P.

Rows 5, 7, 9, and 11: K.

Row 12: K2tog to end.

SATIN LOOP edging

Multiples of 6 sts plus 2 (top edge decreases to two-thirds as many sts)

Row 1: (RS) K2, *bind off 4 sts, leaving last st on RHN, K1, rep from * to end.

Row 2: K2, *yfrn, K2, rep from * to end.

Row 3: K2, *inc1 K in yrn, K2, rep from * to end.

Rows 4–7: K.

SIMPLE LACE edging

Multiples of 5 sts plus 2 (top edge decreases to 4 sts for every multiple, plus 5 instead of 2)

Row 1: (RS) K1, yfwd, *K5, lift 2nd, 3rd, 4th, and 5th sts over first st and off LHN, yfwd, rep from * to last st, K1.

Row 2: K1, *(P1, yon, K1 tbl) into next st, P1, rep from * to end.

Row 3: K2, K1 tbl, *K3, K1 tbl, rep from * to last 2 sts, K2.

Rows 4–6: K.

KNOTTED edging

Multiples of 12 sts

Step 1: Cast on 6 sts and, beg with a K row, work 20 rows in St st. Cut yarn and leave sts on a holder. Make 1 more strip.

Step 2: Make as many sets of 2 strips as required.

Step 3: Slip all strips onto LHN with RS facing. Cross first strip in front of 2nd strip. Bring cast-on edge of 2nd strip in front of first strip, twisting it so RS is still facing, and tuck it between the two strips. Position the cast-on edge behind the sts of the first strip. Knit sts on first strip, each one tog with a loop from the cast-on edge on 2nd strip.

Step 4: Twist rem cast-on edge behind sts on 2nd strip and knit tog as before.

Step 5: Rep to make rem knots.

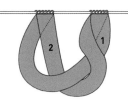

Knit the top of strip 1 to the cast-on edge of strip 2 and the top edge of strip 2 to the bind-off edge of strip 1.

RUFFLED edging

Multiples of 16 sts plus 5 (top edge decreases to 6 sts for every multiple, plus 5)

Row 1: (WS) K5, *P11, K5, rep from * to end.

Row 2: P5, *K2tog, K7, SKP, P5, rep from * to end.

Row 3: K5, *P9, K5, rep from * to end.

Row 4: P5, *K2tog, K5, SKP, P5, rep from * to end.

Row 5: K5, *P7, K5, rep from * to end.

Row 6: P5, *K2tog, K3, SKP, P5, rep from * to end.

Row 7: K5, *P5, K5, rep from * to end.

Row 8: P5, *K2tog, K1, SKP, P5, rep from * to end.

Row 9: K5, *P3, K5, rep from * to end.

Row 10: P5, * SK2P, P5, rep from * to end.

Row 11: K5, *P1, K5, rep from * to end.

LONG LOOP edging

Multiples of 11 sts plus 2 (top edge decreases to 6 sts for every multiple, plus 2)

Row 1: (RS) P.

Row 2: K2, *K1, slip last st back onto LHN, lift next 8 sts over it and off LHN, yrn twice, K into slip st on LHN again, K2, rep from * to end.

Row 3: K1, *P2tog, slip one of the extra loops off LHN, (K1, K1 tbl) twice into rem loop, P1, rep from * to last st, K1.

Rows 4–8: K.

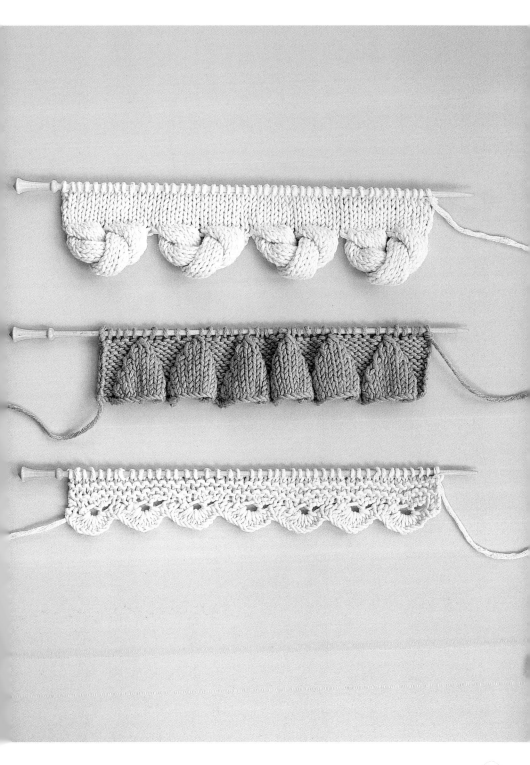

SINGLE frill

Cast on 4 times the finished number of sts required

Row 1: (RS) *K2, lift 2nd st over first st and off RHN, rep from * to end.

Row 2: *P2tog, rep from * to end.

SCALLOP edging

Multiples of 13 sts plus 2 (top edge decreases to 12 sts for every multiple, plus 3 instead of 2)

Row 1: (RS) K1, *K2, SKP, sl2, K3tog, p2sso, K2tog, K2, rep from * to last st, K1.

Row 2: P4, *yrn, P1, yrn, P6, rep from * to last 5 sts, yrn, P1, yrn, P4.

Row 3: K1, yfwd, *K2, SKP, K1, K2tog, K2, yfwd, rep from * to last st, K1.

Row 4: P2, *yrn, P2, yrn, P3, yrn, P2, yrn, P1, rep from * to last st, P1.

Row 5: K2, *yfwd, K1, yfwd, SKP, K1, SK2P, K1, K2tog, (yfwd, K1) twice, rep from * to last st, K1.

Row 6: P.

Row 7: K5, *yfwd, sl2, K3, p2sso, yfwd, K7, rep from * to last 10 sts, yfwd, sl2, K3, p2sso, yfwd, K5.

Rows 8–10: K.

DOUBLE frill

Cast on 4 times the finished number of sts required

Three knitting needles are required

Step 1: Work Single frill (see st pattern at left), followed by 2 rows of St st, and leave on spare needle. Cast on same number of sts and continue with

Step 2:

Row 1: (RS) *K2, lift 2nd st over first st and off RHN, rep from * to end.

Row 2: *P2tog, rep from * to end.

Rows 3, 5, 7, and 9: K.

Rows 4, 6, 8, and 10: P.

Step 3: Keeping the sts on the needles, place the Single frill over the Double frill. Knit the first st on each needle tog. Repeat, knitting both sets of sts tog to the end.

SINGLE frill (top section of picture)
SCALLOP edging (middle section of picture)
DOUBLE frill (bottom section of picture)

118 edgings

FEATHER edging

Cast on 9 sts

Row 1: (RS) sl1, K1, yfwd, K2tog, K1, yfwd, K2tog, yfwd, K2.

Rows 2, 4, 6, and 8: K.

Row 3: sl1, K1, yfwd, K2tog, K2, yfwd, K2tog, yfwd, K2.

Row 5: sl1, K1, yfwd, K2tog, K3, yfwd, K2tog, yfwd, K2.

Row 7: sl1, K1, yfwd, K2tog, K1, yfwd, K2tog, K1, yfwd, K2tog, yfwd, K2.

Row 9: sl1, K1, yfwd, K2tog, K2, yfwd, K2tog, K5.

Row 10: Bind off 4 sts, K to end.

Repeat these 10 rows.

BEADED edging

Cast on 8 sts

Row 1: (RS) sl1, K1, *yfrn, P2tog, (K1, P1, K1) into next st, rep from * once.

Row 2: (K3, yfrn, P2tog) twice, K2.

Row 3: sl1, K1, (yfrn, P2tog, K3) twice.

Row 4: Bind off 2 sts, yfrn, P2tog, bind off next 2 sts, yfrn, P2tog, K2.

Rep these 4 rows.

FERN edging

Cast on 10 sts

Row 1: (RS) sl1, K2, yfwd, K2tog, (yfrn twice, K2tog) twice, K1.

Row 2: sl1, (K2, P1 into 2nd loop of yfrn) twice, K2, yfwd, K2tog, K1.

Row 3: sl1, K2, yfwd, K2tog, K2, (yfrn twice, K2tog) twice, K1.

Row 4: sl1, (K2, P1) twice, K4, yfwd, K2tog, K1.

Row 5: sl1, K2, yfwd, K2tog, K4, (yfrn twice, K2tog) twice, K1.

Row 6: sl1, (K2, P1) twice, K6, yfwd, K2tog, K1.

Row 7: sl1, K2, yfwd, K2tog, K6, (yfrn twice, K2tog) twice, K1.

Row 8: sl1, (K2, P1) twice, K8, yfwd, K2tog, K1.

Row 9: sl1, K2, yfwd, K2tog, K8, (yfrn twice, K2tog) twice, K1.

Row 10: sl1, (K2, P1) twice, K10, yfwd, K2tog, K1.

Row 11: sl1, K2, yfwd, K2tog, K15.

Row 12: Bind off 10 sts, K6, yfwd, K2tog, K1.

Rep these 12 rows.

FEATHER edging (top section of picture)
BEADED edging (middle section of picture)
FERN edging (bottom section of picture)

OPENWORK edging

Cast on 5 sts
Row 1: (RS) sl1, yfwd, K2tog, yfwd, K2.
Row 2 and all WS rows: sl1, K to end.
Row 3: sl1, (yfwd, K2tog) twice, yfwd, K1.
Row 5: sl1, (yfwd, K2tog) twice, yfwd, K2.
Row 7: sl1, (yfwd, K2tog) 3 times, yfwd, K1.
Row 9: sl1, (yfwd, K2tog) 3 times, yfwd, K2.
Row 11: Bind off 6 sts, yfwd, K2tog, yfwd, K1.
Row 12: K.
Rep these 12 rows.

DIAMOND edging

Cast on 10 sts
Row 1: (RS) K5, K2tog, yfwd, K3tog.
Row 2 and all WS rows: yrn to M1, K to end.
Row 3: K4, K2tog, yfwd, K1, yfwd, K2tog.
Row 5: K3, K2tog, yfwd, K3, yfwd, K2tog.
Row 7: K2, K2tog, yfwd, K5, yfwd, K2tog.
Row 9: K4, yfwd, K2tog, K1, K2tog, yfwd, K3tog.
Row 11: K5, yfwd, K3tog, yfwd, K3tog.
Row 12: As row 2.
Rep these 12 rows.

LACY edging

Cast on 18 sts
Row 1: (WS) K6, P7, K5.
Row 2: sl1, K2, yfwd, K2tog, K2, K2tog, yfwd, K5, yfwd, K2tog, (yfwd, K1) twice.
Row 3: K6, yfwd, K2tog, P7, K2, yfwd, K2tog, K1.
Row 4: sl1, K2, yfwd, K2tog, K1, (K2tog, yfwd) twice, K4, yfwd, K2tog, (yfwd, K1) twice, K2.
Row 5: K8, yfwd, K2tog, P7, K2, yfwd, K2tog, K1.
Row 6: sl1, K2, yfwd, K2tog, (K2tog, yfwd) 3 times, K3, yfwd, K2tog, (yfwd, K1) twice, K4.
Row 7: K10, yfwd, K2tog, P7, K2, yfwd, K2tog, K1.
Row 8: sl1, K2, yfwd, K2tog, K1, (K2tog, yfwd) twice, K4, yfwd, K2tog, (yfwd, K1) twice, K6.
Row 9: Bind off 8 sts, K3, yfwd, K2tog, P7, K2, yfwd, K2tog, K1.
Rep rows 2–9.

BERRY edging

Cast on 4 sts
Row 1: (RS) K2, yfwd, K2.
Rows 2, 4, and 6: K.
Row 3: K3, yfwd, K2.
Row 5: K2, yfwd, K2tog, yfwd, K2.
Row 7: K3, yfwd, K2tog, yfwd, K2.
Row 8: Bind off 4 sts, K to end.
Rep these 8 rows.

FAN edging

Cast on 13 sts
Row 1: (RS) sl1, K1, yfwd, K2tog, K5, yfwd, K2tog, yfwd, K2.
Row 2 and all WS rows: yrn to M1, K2tog, K to end.
Row 3: sl1, K1, yfwd, K2tog, K4, (yfwd, K2tog) twice, yfwd, K2.
Row 5: sl1, K1, yfwd, K2tog, K3, (yfwd, K2tog) 3 times, yfwd, K2.
Row 7: sl1, K1, yfwd, K2tog, K2, (yfwd, K2tog) 4 times, yfwd, K2.
Row 9: sl1, K1, yfwd, K2tog, K1, (yfwd, K2tog) 5 times, yfwd, K2.
Row 11: sl1, K1, yfwd, K2tog, K1, K2tog, (yfwd, K2tog) 5 times, K1.
Row 13: sl1, K1, yfwd, K2tog, K2, K2tog, (yfwd, K2tog) 4 times, K1.
Row 15: sl1, K1, yfwd, K2tog, K3, K2tog, (yfwd, K2tog) 3 times, K1.
Row 17: sl1, K1, yfwd, K2tog, K4, K2tog, (yfwd, K2tog) twice, K1.
Row 19: sl1, K1, yfwd, K2tog, K5, K2tog, yfwd, K2tog, K1.
Row 20: As row 2.
Rep these 20 rows.

SPRAY edging

Cast on 11 sts
Row 1: (RS) sl1, K2, yfrn, P2tog, yrn, SKP, (yfwd, SKP) twice.
Row 2: yrn to M1, [P1, (K1, P1) into next st] 3 times, P2, yrn, P2tog, K1 tbl.
Row 3: sl1, K2, yfrn, P2tog, K10.
Row 4: sl1, P11, yrn, P2tog, K1 tbl.
Row 5: sl1, K2, yfrn, P2tog, K10.
Row 6: Bind off 4 sts pwise, P7, yrn, P2tog, K1 tbl.
Rep these 6 rows.

BERRY edging (top section of picture)
FAN edging (middle section of picture)
SPRAY edging (bottom section of picture)

124 edgings

DIAMOND LACE edging

Cast on 9 sts

Row 1 and all RS rows: K.

Row 2: K3, K2tog, yfwd, K2tog, yfwd, K1, yfwd, K1.

Row 4: K2, K2tog, yfwd, K2tog, yfwd, K3, yfwd, K1.

Row 6: K1, K2tog, yfwd, K2tog, yfwd, K5, yfwd, K1.

Row 8: K3, yfwd, K2tog, yfwd, K2tog, K1, K2tog, yfwd, K2tog.

Row 10: K4, yfwd, K2tog, yfwd, K3tog, yfwd, K2tog.

Row 12: K5, yfwd, K3tog, yfwd, K2tog.

Rep these 12 rows.

LOOP AND BRAID edging

Cast on 6 sts

Row 1: (RS) K1, K2tog, yfwd, K2, yfrn, K1.

Row 2: K1, (K1, P1) into yfrn, P2tog, yfwd, K3.

Row 3: K1, K2tog, yfwd, K5.

Row 4: Bind off 2 sts, P2tog, yfwd, K3.

Rep these 4 rows.

GODMOTHER'S edging

Cast on 20 sts

Rows 1, 3, 5, 7, and 9: (RS) K.

Row 2: sl1, K3, (yfwd, K2tog) 7 times, yfwd, K2.

Row 4: sl1, K6, (yfwd, K2tog) 6 times, yfwd, K2.

Row 6: sl1, K9, (yfwd, K2tog) 5 times, yfwd, K2.

Row 8: sl1, K12, (yfwd, K2tog) 4 times, yfwd, K2.

Row 10: sl1, K23.

Row 11: Bind off 4 sts, K20.

Rep rows 2–11.

DIAMOND LACE edging (top section of picture)
LOOP AND BRAID edging (middle section of picture)
GODMOTHER'S edging (bottom section of picture)

LEAF edging

Cast on 6 sts
Row 1: (RS) K3, yfwd, K1, yfwd, K2.
Row 2: P6, inc1 K, K1.
Row 3: K2, P1, K2, yfwd, K1, yfwd, K3.
Row 4: P8, inc1 K, K2.
Row 5: K2, P2, K3, yfwd, K1, yfwd, K4.
Row 6: P10, inc1 K, K3.
Row 7: K2, P3, SKP, K5, K2tog, K1.
Row 8: P8, inc1 K, P1, K3.
Row 9: K2, P1, K1, P2, SKP, K3, K2tog, K1.
Row 10: P6, inc1 K, K1, P1, K3.
Row 11: K2, P1, K1, P3, SKP, K1, K2tog, K1.
Row 12: P4, inc1 K, K2, P1, K3.
Row 13: K2, P1, K1, P4, SK2P, K1.
Row 14: P2tog, bind off 3 sts, K1, P1, K3.
Rep these 14 rows.

CABLE edging

Cast on 8 sts
Row 1: (RS) P3, K4, P1.
Row 2: K1, P4, K3.
Row 3: P3, C4F, P1.
Row 4: K1, P4, K3.
Rep these 4 rows.

SERRATED edging

Cast on 8 sts
Row 1: (RS) K to last 2 sts, inc1 K, yfwd, sl1.
Row 2: K1 tbl, K1, (yfwd, SKP, K1) twice, yfwd, sl1.
Row 3: K1 tbl, K to end, turn and cast on 3 sts.
Row 4: K1 tbl, inc1 K, K2, (yfwd, SKP, K1) twice, yfwd, K1, yfwd, sl1.
Row 5: K1 tbl, K to last 2 sts, inc1 K, yfwd, sl1.
Row 6: K1 tbl, inc1 K, K2, (yfwd, SKP, K1) 3 times, K1, yfwd, sl1.
Row 7: K1 tbl, K to last 2 sts, K2tog.
Row 8: SKP twice, K4, (yfwd, SKP, K1) twice, yfwd, sl1.
Row 9: As row 7.
Row 10: Bind off 3 sts, K2, yfwd, SKP, K1, yfwd, SKP, yfwd, sl1.
Rep rows 3–10.

Ornamental stitches

This collection of stitch patterns delivers another shot of texture—of the more theatrical variety. There are bigger bobbles in profusion and in different configurations, and embossed bells and leaves—some of which are well known for embellishing Aran designs. More fanciful textures take the shape of crazily exuberant loops, huge faux cables, and chunky smocked patterns.

Your knitting will probably grow rather slowly, but these ornamental stitches are not difficult to work. Some of them are rather yarn hungry, though. However, the effects are certainly dramatic and well worth the effort.

BOBBLE stitch
Multiples of 6 sts plus 5
make bobble = K into front and back of same st twice, knit into front of same st; (turn and P5, turn and K5) twice; lift 2nd, 3rd, 4th, and 5th sts over the first st and off RHN
Row 1: (RS) K.
Row 2 and all WS rows: P.
Row 3: K.
Row 5: K5, *make bobble, K5, rep from * to end.
Row 7: K.
Row 9: K.
Row 11: K2, *make bobble, K5, rep from * to last 3 sts, K3.
Row 12: P.
Rep these 12 rows.

POPCORN stitch
Multiples of 6 sts plus 3
Row 1: (RS) K.
Row 2 and all WS rows: P.
Row 3: K1, *(K1, P1, K1) into next st, lift 2nd and 3rd sts over first st, K5, rep from * to last 2 sts, K2.
Row 5: K.
Row 7: K4, *(K1, P1, K1) into next st, lift 2nd and 3rd sts over first st, K5, rep from * to last 5 sts, K5.
Row 8: P.
Rep these 8 rows.

HAZELNUT stitch
Multiples of 4 sts plus 3
Row 1: (RS) *P3, (K1, yfwd, K1) into next st, rep from * to last 3 sts, P3.
Row 2: K3, *P3, K3, rep from * to end.
Row 3: *P3, K3, rep from * to last 3 sts, P3.
Row 4: K3, *P3tog, K3, rep from * to end.
Row 5: P.
Row 6: K.
Row 7: P1, *(K1, yfwd, K1) in next st, P3, rep from * to last 2 sts, *(K1, yfwd, K1) in next st, P1.
Row 8: K1, *P3, K3, rep from * to last 4 sts, P3, K1.
Row 9: P1, *K3, P3, rep from * to last 4 sts, K3, P1.
Row 10: K1, *P3tog, K3, rep from * to last 4 sts, P3tog, K1.
Row 11: P.
Row 12: K.
Rep these 12 rows.

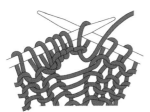

Bobble stitch 1 Knit into the front and back of the next stitch twice, and then into the front again.

Bobble stitch 2 Lift the second, third, fourth, and fifth stitches over the first and off the RHN to complete the bobble.

BOBBLE stitch (left section of picture)
POPCORN stitch (middle section of picture)
HAZELNUT stitch (right section of picture)

DAISY stitch

Multiples of 10 sts plus 8

make daisy = K into loop 3 rows below 2nd st on LHN, pull up loop, (K2, pull next loop through same st) twice

Rows 1, 3, and 5: (RS) K.

Rows 2, 4, and 6: P.

Row 7: K2, make daisy, *K6, make daisy, rep from * to last 2 sts, K2.

Row 8: P2, *(P2tog, P1) twice, P2tog, P5, rep from * to last 9 sts, (P2tog, P1) 3 times.

Rows 9, 11, and 13: K.

Rows 10, 12, and 14: P.

Row 15: K7, *make daisy, K6, rep from * to last st, K1.

Row 16: P2, *P5, (P2tog, P1) twice, P2tog, rep from * to last 6 sts, P6.

Rep these 16 rows.

BELL motif

Motif of 6 sts on Reverse St st background

Row 1: (RS) P to cluster position, cast on 6 sts, P to end.

Row 2 and all WS rows: K background, P cast-on cluster, K to end.

Row 3: P background, K cluster, P to end.

Row 5: P background, SKP, K2, K2tog, P to end.

Row 7: P background, SKP, K2tog, P to end.

Row 9: P background, K2tog, P to end.

Row 11: P background, P2tog, P to end.

Row 12: K.

Rep these 12 rows.

EMBOSSED LEAF motif

Motif of 9 sts on Reverse St st background

Row 1: (RS) P to leaf position, yon, K1, yfrn, P to end.

Row 2 and all WS rows: K background, P cast-on cluster, K to end.

Row 3: P background, K1, (yfwd, K1) twice, P to end.

Row 5: P background, K2, yfwd, K1, yfwd, K2, P to end.

Row 7: P background, K3, yfwd, K1, yfwd, K3, P to end.

Row 9: P background, SKP, K5, K2tog, P to end.

Row 11: P background, SKP, K3, K2tog, P to end.

Row 13: P background, SKP, K1, K2tog, P to end.

Row 15: P background, SK2P, P to end.

Row 16: K.

Rep these 16 rows.

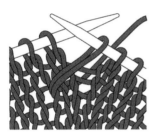

Knit into the loop three rows below the second stitch.

Work three long loops for the daisy, knitting two stitches between the loops.

DAISY stitch (top section of picture)

BELL motif (middle section of picture)

EMBOSSED LEAF motif (bottom section of picture)

KNOTTED MOCK cable

Panel of 30 sts on Reverse St st background

A spare needle and 2 safety pins are required

Row 1: (RS) (K1 tbl twice, P2) 3 times, P6, (P2, K1 tbl twice) 3 times.

Row 2: (P1 tbl twice, K2) 3 times, K6, (K2, P1 tbl twice) 3 times.

Rows 3–16: Rep rows 1 and 2 seven more times.

Next work the knotted cable.

Step 1: (K1 tbl twice, P2) twice, K1 tbl twice. Leave rem sts on spare needle. Turn work and cont in pattern for 11 more rows. Leave sts on safety pin A.

Step 2: Keep next 10 Reverse St sts on spare needle and leave at back of work.

Step 3: Join yarn to final batch of sts. Work in pattern for 20 rows. Leave sts on safety pin B.

Step 4: Pass left rib, B, over and under right rib, A, to make knot.

Step 5: Slip rib A sts, Reverse St sts, and then rib B sts onto LHN.

Rows 17–24: Rep rows 1 and 2 four times.

Rep these 24 rows.

BOBBLE brocade

Multiples of 6 sts plus 2
Row 1: (RS) P2, *K1, P2, rep from * to end.
Row 2: K2, *P1, K2, rep from * to end.
Row 3: P2, *K1, P2, (P1, K1, P1, K1) into next st, P2, rep from * to end.
Row 4: K2, *P4, K2, P1, K2, rep from * to end.
Row 5: P2, *K1, P2, K4, turn and K4, turn and P4, P2, rep from * to end.
Row 6: K2, *P4tog, K2, P1, K2, rep from * to end.
Row 7: As row 1.
Row 8: As row 2.
Row 9: P2, *(P1, K1, P1, K1) into next st, P2, K1, P2, rep from * to end.
Row 10: K2, *P1, K2, P4, K2, rep from * to end.
Row 11: P2, *P4, turn and K4, turn and P4, P2, K1, P2, rep from * to end.
Row 12: K2, *P1, K2, P4tog, K2, rep from * to end.
Rep these 12 rows.

HOLLOW OAK with bobbles

Panel of 15 sts on Reverse St st background
make bobble = K into front and back of same st twice, knit into front of same st; (turn and P5, turn and K5) twice; lift 2nd, 3rd, 4th, and 5th sts over the first st and off RHN
T3B = slip 1 st onto CN and hold at back of work, K2, P1 from CN
T3F = slip 2 sts onto CN and hold at front of work, P1, K2 from CN
Rows 1, 3, 5, and 7: (WS) K5, P5, K5.
Row 2: P5, K2, make bobble, K2, P5.
Row 4: P5, make bobble, K3, make bobble, P5.
Row 6: As row 2.
Row 8: P4, T3B, P1, T3F, P4.
Row 9: K4, P2, K1, P1, K1, P2, K4.
Row 10: P3, T3B, K1, P1, K1, T3F, P3.
Row 11: K3, P3, K1, P1, K1, P3, K3.
Row 12: P2, T3B, (P1, K1) twice, P1, T3F, P2.
Row 13: K2, P2, (K1, P1) 3 times, K1, P2, K2.
Row 14: P2, K3, (P1, K1) twice, P1, K3, P2.
Row 15: As row 13.
Row 16: P2, T3F, (P1, K1) twice, P1, T3B, P2.
Row 17: As row 11.
Row 18: P3, T3F, K1, P1, K1, T3B, P3.
Row 19: As row 9.
Row 20: P4, T3F, P1, T3B, P4.
Rep these 20 rows.

SMOCKED honeycomb

Multiples of 12 sts plus 1
tie 5 = slip next 5 sts onto CN, wrap yarn around sts twice counterclockwise, (K1, P3, K1) from CN
Row 1: (RS) (K1, P3) 3 times, K1.
Row 2 and all WS rows: (P1, K3) 3 times, P1.
Row 3: tie 5, P3, tie 5.
Row 5: As row 1.
Row 7: K1, P3, tie 5, P3, K1.
Row 8: As row 2.
Rep these 8 rows.

WHEATEAR pattern

Multiples of 11 sts plus 2

make bobble = K into front and back of same st twice, K into front of same st; (turn and P5, turn and K5) twice; lift 2nd, 3rd, 4th, and 5th sts over the first st and off RHN

Row 1: (RS) K1, *K5, yfwd, K1, yfwd, K3, K2tog, rep from * to last st, K1.

Rows 2, 4, 6, and 8: P1, *P2tog, P10, rep from * to last st, P1.

Row 3: K1, *K6, yfwd, K1, yfwd, K2, K2tog, rep from * to last st, K1.

Row 5: K1, *K7, (yfwd, K1) twice, K2tog, rep from * to last st, K1.

Row 7: K1, *K8, yfwd, K1, yfwd, K2tog, rep from * to last st, K1.

Row 9: K1, * SKP, K4, yfwd, K1, yfwd, K2, make bobble, K1, rep from * to last st, K1.

Row 10: P1, *P1, P1 tbl, P8, P2tog tbl, rep from * to last st, P1.

Row 11: K1, * SKP, K3, yfwd, K1, yfwd, K5, rep from * to last st, K1.

Rows 12, 14, 16, and 18: P1, *P10, P2tog tbl, rep from * to last st, P1.

Row 13: K1, * SKP, K2, yfwd, K1, yfwd, K6, rep from * to last st, K1.

Row 15: K1, * SKP, (K1, yfwd) twice, K7, rep from * to last st, K1.

Row 17: K1, * SKP, yfwd, K1, yfwd, K8, rep from * to last st, K1.

Row 19: K1, *K1, make bobble, K2, yfwd, K1, yfwd, K4, K2tog, rep from * to last st, K1.

Row 20: P1, *P2tog, P8, P1 tbl, P1, rep from * to last st, P1.

Rep these 20 rows.

BOBBLE SCALLOPS pattern

Multiples of 20 sts plus 2

make bobble = K into front and back of same st 3 times, lift 2nd, 3rd, 4th, 5th, and then 6th sts over the first st and off RHN

Row 1: (RS) K1, *inc1 K, (make bobble, P3) 4 times, make bobble but return first st to LHN and inc1 K, rep from * to last st, K1.

Row 2: P1, *P2, (K3, P1) 4 times, P2, rep from * to last st, P1.

Row 3: K1, *K1, inc1 K, (K1, P3) 4 times, inc1 K, K1, rep from * to last st, K1.

Row 4: P1, *P3, (K3, P1) 4 times, P3, rep from * to last st, P1.

Row 5: K1, *K2, inc1 K, (K1, P3) 4 times, inc1 K, K2, rep from * to last st, K1.

Row 6: P1, *P4, (K3, P1) 4 times, P4, rep from * to last st, P1.

Row 7: K1, *K3, inc1 K, (K1, P2tog, P1) 4 times, inc1 K, K3, rep from * to last st, K1.

Row 8: P1, *P5, (K2, P1) 4 times, P5, rep from * to last st, P1.

Row 9: K1, *K4, inc1 K, (K1, P2tog) 4 times, inc1 K, K4, rep from * to last st, K1.

Row 10: P1, *P6, (K1, P1) 4 times, P6, rep from * to last st, P1.

Row 11: K1, *K5, inc1 K, K1, K2tog 3 times, K into front and back of next 2 sts tog, K5, rep from * to last st, K1.

Row 12: P.

Rep these 12 rows.

WHEATEAR pattern (top section of picture)
BOBBLE SCALLOPS pattern (bottom section of picture)

LOOP stitch

Multiples of 2 sts plus 1

make loop = insert RHN into next st, yon and around two LH fingers, yrn again, pull 2 loops through st and slip on LHN, K2tog tbl, gently pull the long loop to secure it

Rows 1 and 3: (RS) K.

Row 2: K1, *make loop, K1, rep from * to end.

Row 4: K2, *make loop, K1, rep from * to last st, K1.

Rep these 4 rows.

Wrap the yarn over the RHN, around two fingers, and over the RHN again.

Pull the two loops through.

BIND-OFF fringe

Multiples of 2 sts plus 1

make fringe = cast on 4 sts, bind off same 4 sts

Row 1: (RS) K.

Row 2: K.

Row 3: K1, *make fringe, K1, rep from * to end.

Row 4: P1, K1, rep from * to last st, P1.

Rows 5 and 6: K.

Row 7: *make fringe, K1, rep from * to last st, make fringe.

Row 8: *K1, P1, rep from * to last st, K1.

Rep these 8 rows.

CHAIN STITCH loops

Multiples of 2 sts plus 1

A crochet hook is required

make loop = K next st but leave on LHN; insert crochet hook into same st from front to back; pull loop through, leave on hook and drop st from LHN; make 12 chain sts; keeping chain at front and yarn at back of work, slip loop onto RHN and remove hook, slip last K st over loop

Row 1: (RS) K.

Row 2 and all WS rows: P.

Row 3: K1, *make loop, K1, rep from * to end.

Row 5: K.

Row 7: K1, *K1, make loop, rep from * to last 2 sts, K2.

Row 8: P.

Rep these 8 rows.

LOOP stitch (top section of picture)
BIND-OFF fringe (middle section of picture)
CHAIN STITCH loops (bottom section of picture)

NOSEGAY panel

Panel of 14 sts on Reverse St st background

make bobble = K into front and back of same st twice, K into front of same st; (turn and P5, turn and K5) twice; lift 2nd, 3rd, 4th, and 5th sts over the first st and off RHN

T2B = K 2nd st on LHN tfl, then P first st and slip both off LHN

T2F = P 2nd st on LHN tbl, then K first st and slip both off LHN

Row 1: (WS) K6, P2, K6.
Row 2: P5, C2B, C2F, P5.
Row 3: K4, T2F, P2, T2B, K4.
Row 4: P3, T2B, C2B, C2F, T2F, P3.
Row 5: K2, T2F, K1, P4, K1, T2B, K2.
Row 6: P1, T2B, P1, T2B, K2, T2F, P1, T2F, P1.
Row 7: K1, P1, K2, P1, K1, P2, K1, P1, K2, P1, K1.
Row 8: P1, make bobble, P1, T2B, P1, K2, P1, T2F, P1, make bobble, P1.
Row 9: K3, P1, K2, P2, K2, P1, K3.
Row 10: P3, make bobble, P2, K2, P2, make bobble, P3.
Rep these 10 rows.

SMOCKING

Panel of 14 sts on Reverse St st background

tie 6 = slip next 6 sts onto CN, wrap yarn around sts twice counterclockwise, (K2, P2, K2) from CN

Row 1: (RS) (K2, P2) 3 times, K2.
Row 2 and all WS rows : (P2, K2) 3 times, P2.
Row 3: tie 6, P2, tie 6.
Row 5: As row 1.
Row 7: K2, P2, tie 6, P2, K2.
Row 8: (P2, K2) 3 times, P2.
Rep these 8 rows.

GRAPES panel

Panel of 11 sts on Reverse St st background

make bobble = K into front and back of same st twice, K into front of same st; (turn and P5, turn and K5) twice; lift 2nd, 3rd, 4th, and 5th sts over the first st and off RHN

Row 1: (RS) K1, (P4, K1) twice.
Row 2: P1, (K4, P1) twice.
Row 3: K1, P4, make bobble, P4, K1.
Row 4: P1, K4, P1 tbl, K4, P1.
Row 5: K1, P3, make bobble, P1, make bobble, P3, K1.
Row 6: P1, K3, P1 tbl, K1, P1 tbl, K3, P1.
Row 7: K1, P2, (make bobble, P1) twice, make bobble, P2, K1.
Row 8: P1, K2, (P1 tbl, K1) twice, P1 tbl, K2, P1.
Rep these 8 rows.

NOSEGAY panel (left section of picture)
SMOCKING (middle section of picture)
GRAPES panel (right section of picture)

(142) ornamental stitches

Eyelet patterns

Eyelets produce an open effect using yarn-over increases matched by an equal number of decreased stitches, usually in pairs—the same technique as for knitted lace. The difference lies in the proportion of open areas to background; eyelet patterns have distinct eyelets surrounded by a Stockinette stitch background while lace is much more open and often has a Garter stitch background. The technique is very simple and just two or four rows will produce many effective patterns. Always knit or purl the yarn over that makes the eyelet through the back of the stitch on the return row to keep the eyelet open.

The patterns usually benefit from being well stretched, so block the finished pieces as well as the gauge swatches before measuring them. The delicate appearance of eyelet patterns such as Butterfly and Quatrefoil eyelets has probably led to their popularity for babies' garments and linens. Finer yarns certainly suit the patterns well, and very fine Shetland wool could be used to knit Cat's Paw and Snowflake eyelets, for example, to create exquisite shawls and scarves. However, the more geometric shapes of squares, diamonds, and triangles are just as suitable for summery fashions in medium-weight cotton yarns.

SNOWDROP eyelets
Multiples of 5 sts plus 2
Row 1: (RS) P2, *K3, P2, rep from * to end.
Row 2 and all WS rows: *K2, P3, rep from * to last 2 sts, K2.
Row 3: As row 1.
Row 5: P2, *yfwd, SK2P, yfwd, P2, rep from * to end.
Row 6: As row 2.
Rep these 6 rows.

SNOWFLAKE eyelets
Multiples of 6 sts plus 1
Row 1: (RS) K1, *yfwd, SKP, K1, K2tog, yfwd, K1, rep from * to end.
Row 2 and all WS rows: P.
Row 3: K2, yfwd, *K3, yfwd, rep from * to last 2 sts, K2.
Row 5: K2tog, yfwd, SKP, K1, K2tog, yfwd, *SK2P, yfwd, SKP, K1, K2tog, yfwd, rep from * to last 2 sts, SKP.
Row 7: K1, *K2tog, yfwd, K1, yfwd, SKP, K1, rep from * to end.
Row 9: As row 3.
Row 11: K1, *K2tog, yfwd, SK2P, yfwd, SKP, K1, rep from * to end.
Row 12: P.
Rep these 12 rows.

VANDYKE eyelet rows
Multiples of 8 sts plus 2
Row 1: (RS) K1, *K5, yfwd, K2tog, K1, rep from * to last st, K1.
Row 2 and all WS rows: P.
Row 3: K1, *K3, K2tog tbl, yfwd, K1, yfwd, K2tog, rep from * to last st, K1.
Row 5: K2, *K1, K2tog tbl, yfwd, K3, yfwd, K2tog, rep from * to end.
Row 7: K1, *yfwd, K2tog tbl and return st to LHN, pass next st over it and slip onto RHN, yfwd, K5, rep from * to last st, K1.
Row 9: K.
Row 10: P.
Rep these 10 rows.

SNOWDROP eyelets (top section of picture)
SNOWFLAKE eyelets (middle section of picture)
VANDYKE eyelet rows (bottom section of picture)

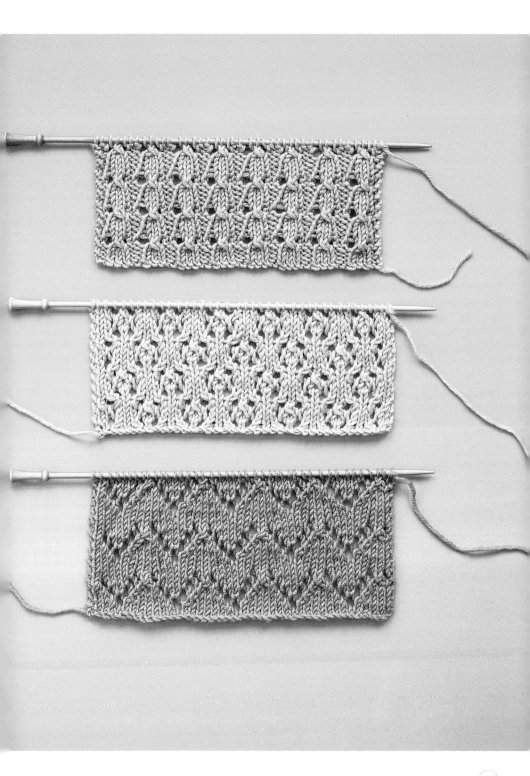

DIAMOND eyelet boxes

Multiples of 14 sts plus 11

Row 1: (RS) K2, P7, *K3, yfwd, SKP, K2, P7, rep from * to last 2 sts, K2.

Rows 2, 4, 6, 8, and 10: P2, K7, *P7, K7, rep from * to last 2 sts, P2.

Row 3: K2, P7, *K1, K2tog, yfwd, K1, yfwd, SKP, K1, P7, rep from * to last 2 sts, K2.

Row 5: K2, P7, *K2tog, yfwd, K3, yfwd, SKP, P7, rep from * to last 2 sts, K2.

Row 7: K2, P7, *K2, yfwd, SK2P, yfwd, K2, P7, rep from * to last 2 sts, K2.

Row 9: As row 1.

Row 11: P2, K3, yfwd, SKP, K2, *P7, K3, yfwd, SKP, K2, rep from * to last 2 sts, P2.

Rows 12, 14, 16, and 18: K2, P7, *K7, P7, rep from * to last 2 sts, K2.

Row 13: P2, K1, K2tog, yfwd, K1, yfwd, SKP, K1, *P7, K1, K2tog, yfwd, K1, yfwd, SKP, K1, rep from * to last 2 sts, P2.

Row 15: P2, K2tog, yfwd, K3, yfwd, SKP, *P7, K2tog, yfwd, K3, yfwd, SKP, rep from * to last 2 sts, P2.

Row 17: P2, K2, yfwd, SK2P, yfwd, K2, *P7, K2, yfwd, SK2P, yfwd, K2, rep from * to last 2 sts, P2.

Row 19: As row 11.

Row 20: K2, P7, *K7, P7, rep from * to last 2 sts, K2.

Rep these 20 rows.

SYCAMORE eyelets

Multiples of 6 sts plus 3

Rows 1 and 3: (RS) K.

Row 2 and all WS rows: P.

Row 5: *K4, yfwd, SKP, rep from * to last 3 sts, K3.

Row 7: K2, K2tog, yfwd, K1, yfwd, SKP, *K1, K2tog, yfwd, K1, yfwd, SKP, rep from * to last 2 sts, K2.

Rows 9 and 11: K.

Row 13: K1, yfwd, SKP, *K4, yfwd, SKP, rep from * to end.

Row 15: K2, yfwd, SKP, K1, K2tog, yfwd, * K1, yfwd, SKP, K1, K2tog, yfwd, rep from * to last 2 sts, K2.

Row 16: P.

Rep these 16 rows.

EYELET rows

Multiples of 2 sts plus 1

Row 1: (RS) K.

Rows 2 and 3: K.

Row 4: K1, *yfwd, SKP, rep from * to end.

Rep these 4 rows.

TIP This pattern tends to distort over large areas.

QUATREFOIL eyelets

Multiples of 8 sts

Row 1 and all WS rows: P.

Row 2: K.

Row 4: K3, *yfwd, SKP, K6, rep from * to last 5 sts, yfwd, SKP, K3.

Row 6: K1, *K2tog, yfwd, K1, yfwd, SKP, K3, rep from * to last 7 sts, K2tog, yfwd, K1, yfwd, SKP, K2.

Row 8: As row 4.

Row 10: K.

Row 12: K7, *yfwd, SKP, K6, rep from * to last st, K1.

Row 14: K5, *K2tog, yfwd, K1, yfwd, SKP, K3, rep from * to last 3 sts, K3.

Row 16: As row 12.

Rep these 16 rows.

GARTER eyelet diamonds

Multiples of 16 sts

Row 1: (RS) *K6, K2tog, yfwd, K1, yfwd, K2tog, K5, rep from * to end.

Rows 2 and all WS rows: K.

Row 3: *K5, K2tog, yfwd, K3, yfwd, K2tog, K4, rep from * to end.

Row 5: *K4, K2tog, yfwd, K5, yfwd, K2tog, K3, rep from * to end.

Row 7: *K3, K2tog, yfwd, K7, yfwd, K2tog, K2, rep from * to end.

Row 9: *K2, K2tog, yfwd, K9, yfwd, K2tog, K1, rep from * to end.

Row 11: *K1, K2tog, yfwd, K11, yfwd, K2tog, rep from * to end.

Row 13: *K1, yfwd, K2tog, K11, K2tog, yfwd, rep from * to end.

Row 15: *K2, yfwd, K2tog, K9, K2tog, yfwd, K1, rep from * to end.

Row 17: *K3, yfwd, K2tog, K7, K2tog, yfwd, K2, rep from * to end.

Row 19: *K4, yfwd, K2tog, K5, K2tog, yfwd, K3, rep from * to end.

Row 21: *K5, yfwd, K2tog, K3, K2tog, yfwd, K4, rep from * to end.

Row 23: *K6, yfwd, K2tog, K1, K2tog, yfwd, K5, rep from * to end.

Row 24: K.

Rep these 24 rows.

EYELET squares

Multiples of 16 sts plus 1

Row 1 and all WS rows: P.

Rows 2, 4, 6, and 8: K1, *K8, (yfwd, SKP) 4 times, rep from * to end.

Rows 10, 12, 14, and 16: K1, *(yfwd, SKP) 4 times, K8, rep from * to end.

Rep these 16 rows.

BUTTERFLY eyelets

Multiples of 10 sts plus 1

Rows 1 and 3: (RS) *K1, yfwd, SKP, K5, K2tog, yfwd, rep from * to last st, K1.

Rows 2 and 4: P1, *P9, sl1, rep from * to end.

Row 5: K.

Row 6: P.

Row 7: *K3, K2tog, yfwd, K1, yfwd, SKP, K2, rep from * to last st, K1.

Row 8: P1 *P4, sl1, P5, rep from * to end.

Row 9: As row 7.

Row 10: As row 8.

Row 11: K.

Row 12: P.

Rep these 12 rows.

DIAMOND eyelets

Multiples of 8 sts plus 1

Row 1: (RS) K1, *K1, K2tog, yfwd, K1, yfwd, K2tog, K2, rep from * to end.

Row 2 and all WS rows: P.

Row 3: K1, *K2tog, yfwd, K3, yfwd, K2tog, K1, rep from * to end.

Row 5: K2tog, *yfwd, K5, yfwd, SK2P, rep from * to last 8 sts, yfwd, K5, yfwd, K2tog.

Row 7: K1, *yfwd, K2tog, K3, K2tog, yfwd, K1, rep from * to end.

Row 9: K1, *K1, yfwd, K2tog, K1, K2tog, yfwd, K2, rep from * to end.

Row 11: K1, *K2, yfwd, SK2P, yfwd, K3, rep from * to end.

Row 12: P.

Rep these 12 rows.

FLYING eyelets

Multiples of 11 sts plus 2

Row 1 and all WS rows: P.

Row 2: K6, *yfwd, SKP, K9, rep from * to last 7 sts, yfwd, SKP, K5.

Row 4: K7, *yfwd, SKP, K9, rep from * to last 6 sts, yfwd, SKP, K4.

Row 6: K3, *K2tog, yfwd, K3, yfwd, SKP, K4, rep from * to last 10 sts, K2tog, yfwd, K3, yfwd, SKP, K3.

Row 8: *K2, K2tog, yfwd, K5, yfwd, SKP, rep from * to last 2 sts, K2.

Row 10: K1, *K2tog, yfwd, K9, rep from * to last st, K1.

Row 12: *K2tog, yfwd, K9, rep from * to last 2 sts, K2.

Rep these 12 rows.

BUTTERFLY eyelets (top section of picture)
DIAMOND eyelets (middle section of picture)
FLYING eyelets (bottom section of picture)

150 eyelet patterns

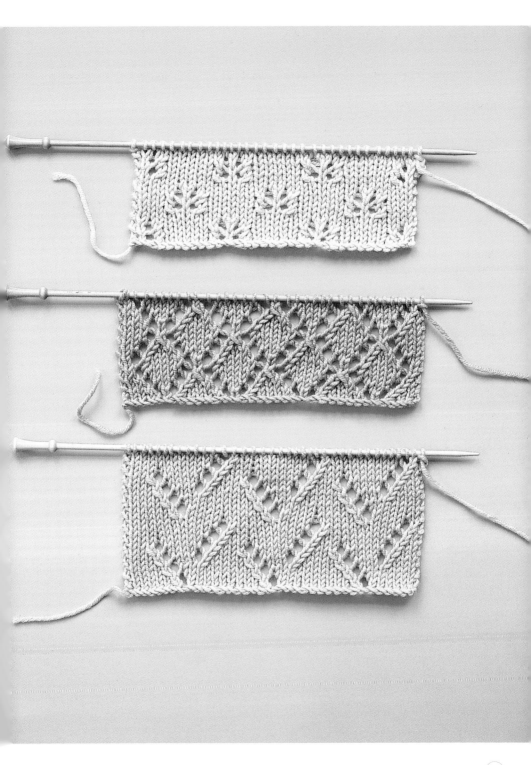

LATTICE insertion

Panel of 7 sts on Garter st background

Row 1: (RS) (K2tog, yfwd) 3 times, K1.

Row 2: P.

Row 3: K1, (K2tog, yfwd) twice, K2.

Row 4: P.

Rep these 4 rows.

SCALLOP insertion

Panel of 10 sts

Row 1: (RS) P5, yon, K1, P2, K1, yfrn, P5.

Row 2: P5, yrn, P2, K2, P2, yrn, P5.

Row 3: P5, yon, K3, P2, K3, yfrn, P5.

Row 4: P5, yrn, P4, K2, P4, yrn, P5.

Row 5: P5, K5, P2, K5, P5.

Row 6: P10, K2, P10.

Row 7: P5, ybk, SKP, K3, P2, K3, K2tog, P5.

Row 8: P5, P2tog, P2, K2, P2, P2tog tbl, P5.

Row 9: P5, ybk, SKP, K1, P2, K1, K2tog, P5.

Row 10: P5, P2tog, K2, P2tog tbl, P5.

Rep these 10 rows.

ZIGZAG insertion

Panel of 5 sts on Reverse St st background

Row 1: (RS) K.

Row 2 and all WS rows: P.

Row 3: K1, K2tog, yfwd, K2.

Row 5: K2tog, yfwd, K3.

Row 7: K.

Row 9: K2, yfwd, SKP, K1.

Row 11: K3, yfwd, SKP.

Row 12: P.

Rep these 12 rows.

LATTICE insertion (left section of picture)
SCALLOP insertion (middle section of picture)
ZIGZAG insertion (right section of picture)

BLUEBELL eyelets

Multiples of 14 sts
Row 1: (RS) *P2, K3 tbl, P4, K3 tbl, P2, rep from * to end.
Row 2: *K2, P3 tbl, K4, P3 tbl, K2, rep from * to end.
Row 3: *P2, K3 tbl, P4, yon, SK2P, yfrn, P2, rep from * to end.
Row 4: *K2, P1, P1 tbl, P1, K4, P3 tbl, K2, rep from * to end.
Row 5: As row 1.
Row 6: As row 2.
Row 7: *P2, yon, SK2P, yfrn, P4, K3 tbl, P2, rep from * to end.
Row 8: *K2, P3 tbl, K4, P1, P1 tbl, P1, K2, rep from * to end.
Rep these 8 rows.

PEAPOD eyelets

Multiples of 12 sts plus 2
Row 1: (RS) K.
Row 2: P.
Row 3: K4, K2tog, K1, yfwd, *K9, K2tog, K1, yfwd, rep from * to last 7 sts, K7.
Row 4: P8, yrn, P1, P2tog, *P9, yrn, P1, P2tog, rep from * to last 3 sts, P3.
Row 5: K2, *K2tog, K1, yfwd, K9, rep from * to end.
Row 6: P10, yrn, P1, P2tog, *P9, yrn, P1, P2tog, rep from * to last st, P1.
Row 7: K.
Row 8: P.
Row 9: K7, yfwd, K1, SKP, *K9, yfwd, K1, SKP, rep from * to last 4 sts, K4.
Row 10: P3, P2tog tbl, P1, yrn, *P9, P2tog tbl, P1, yrn, rep from * to last 8 sts, P8.
Row 11: *K9, yfwd, K1, SKP, rep from * to last 2 sts, K2.
Row 12: P1, P2tog tbl, P1, yrn, *P9, P2tog tbl, P1, yrn, rep from * to last 10 sts, P10.
Rep these 12 rows.

LADDER eyelets

Multiples of 14 sts plus 11
Row 1: (RS) K2tog, K3, yfwd, *K1, yfwd, K3, K2tog tbl, yfwd, SK2P, yfwd, K2tog, K3, yfwd, rep from * to last 6 sts, K1, yfwd, K3, K2tog tbl.
Row 2: P.
Rep these 2 rows.

CLOVERLEAF eyelets
Multiples of 8 sts plus 7
Row 1: (RS) K.
Row 2 and all WS rows: P.
Row 3: K2, yfwd, SK2P, yfwd, *K5, yfwd, SK2P, yfwd, rep from * to last 2 sts, K2.
Row 5: K3, yfwd, SKP, *K6, yfwd, SKP, rep from * to last 2 sts, K2.
Row 7: K.
Row 9: K1, *K5, yfwd, SK2P, yfwd, rep from * to last 6 sts, K6.
Row 11: K7, *yfwd, SKP, K6, rep from * to end.
Row 12: P.
Rep these 12 rows.

PINECONE eyelets
Multiples of 10 sts plus 1
Row 1: (RS) K.
Row 2 and all WS rows: P.
Row 3: K3, K2tog, yfwd, K1, yfwd, SKP, *K5, K2tog, yfwd, K1, yfwd, SKP, rep from * to last 3 sts, K3.
Row 5: K2, K2tog, yfwd, K3, yfwd, SKP, *K3, K2tog, yfwd, K3, yfwd, SKP, rep from * to last 2 sts, K2.
Rows 7 and 9: As row 3.
Row 11: K.
Row 13: K1, *yfwd, SKP, K5, K2tog, yfwd, K1, rep from * to end.
Row 15: K2, yfwd, SKP, K3, K2tog, yfwd, *K3, yfwd, SKP, K3, K2tog, yfwd, rep from * to last 2 sts, K2.
Rows 17 and 19: As row 13.
Row 20: P.
Rep these 20 rows.

ROSARY stitch
Multiples of 8 sts plus 1
Rows 1 and 3: (RS) K1, *yfwd, K2, SK2P, K2, yfwd, K1, rep from * to end.
Row 2 and all WS rows: P.
Rows 5 and 7: K2tog, *K2, yfwd, K1, yfwd, K2, SK2P, rep from *, ending last rep sl1, K1.
Row 8: P.
Rep these 8 rows.

CAT'S PAW eyelets

Multiples of 12 sts plus 1

Row 1: (RS) *K1, yfwd, SKP, K7, K2tog, yfwd, rep from * to last st, K1.

Row 2 and all WS rows: P.

Row 3: *K2, yfwd, SKP, K5, K2tog, yfwd, K1, rep from * to last st, K1.

Row 5: As row 1.

Row 7: *K4, K2tog, yfwd, K1, yfwd, SKP, K3, rep from * to last st, K1.

Row 9: *K3, K2tog, yfwd, K3, yfwd, SKP, K2, rep from * to last st, K1.

Row 11: As row 7.

Row 12: P.

Rep these 12 rows.

EYELET triangles

Multiples of 10 sts plus 7

Row 1: (RS) *K2, (yfwd, SKP) 4 times, rep from * to last 7 sts, K7.

Row 2 and all WS rows: P.

Row 3: *K3, (yfwd, SKP) 3 times, K1, rep from * to last 7 sts, K7.

Row 5: *K4, (yfwd, SKP) twice, K2, rep from * to last 7 sts, K7.

Row 7: *K5, yfwd, SKP, K3, rep from * to last 7 sts, K7.

Row 9: K5, *K2, (yfwd, SKP) 4 times, rep from * to last 2 sts, K2.

Row 11: K5, *K3, (yfwd, SKP) 3 times, K1, rep from * to last 2 sts, K2.

Row 13: K5, *K4, (yfwd, SKP) twice, K2, rep from * to last 2 sts, K2.

Row 15: K5, *K5, yfwd, SKP, K3, rep from * to last 2 sts, K2.

Row 16: P.

Rep these 16 rows.

VANDYKE eyelets

Multiples of 10 sts plus 1

Row 1: (RS) K1, * yfwd, SKP, K8, rep from * to end.

Row 2 and all WS rows: P.

Row 3: K1, *K1, yfwd, SKP, K5, K2tog, yfwd, rep from * to end.

Row 5: K1, *K2, yfwd, SKP, K3, K2tog, yfwd, K1, rep from * to end.

Row 7: K1, *K5, yfwd, SKP, K3, rep from * to end.

Row 9: K1, *K3, K2tog, yfwd, K1, yfwd, SKP, K2, rep from * to end.

Row 11: K1, *K2, K2tog, yfwd, K3, yfwd, SKP, K1, rep from * to end.

Row 12: P.

Rep these 12 rows.

CAT'S PAW eyelets (top section of picture)
EYELET triangles (middle section of picture)
VANDYKE eyelets (bottom section of picture)

EYELET MOCK cable

Multiples of 7 sts plus 2

Row 1: (RS) *P2, yon, SKP, K3, rep from * to last 2 sts, P2.
Row 2: *K2, P2, P2tog tbl, yrn, P1, rep from * to last 2 sts, K2.
Row 3: *P2, K2, yfwd, SKP, K1, rep from * to last 2 sts, P2.
Row 4: *K2, P2tog tbl, yrn, P3, rep from * to last 2 sts, K2.
Row 5: *P2, K5, rep from * to last 2 sts, P2.
Row 6: *K2, P5, rep from * to last 2 sts, K2.
Rep these 6 rows.

CROSSED RIBS with faggoting

Multiples of 6 sts plus 2

Row 1 and all WS rows: K2, *P2tog, yrn, P1 tbl, P1, K2, rep from * to end.
Rows 2, 4, 6, 8, and 10: P2, *SKP, yfwd, K2, P2, rep from * to end.
Row 12: P2, *slip 2 sts onto CN and hold at front of work, SKP, yfwd, K2 from CN, P2, rep from * to end.
Rep these 12 rows.

DIAMOND eyelet insertion

Panel of 10 sts on Reverse St st background

Row 1: (RS) K2, K2tog, yfwd, K2tog but leave on LHN, K into first st again and slip both off LHN, yfwd, SKP, K2.
Rows 2 and 4: P.
Row 3: K1, K2tog, yfwd, K4, yfwd, SKP, K1.
Row 5: K2tog, yfwd, K1, K2tog, yfrn to make 2 sts, SKP, K1, yfwd, SKP.
Row 6: P4, K1, P5.
Row 7: K2, yfwd, SKP, K2, K2tog, yfwd, K2.
Row 8: P.
Row 9: K3, yfwd, SKP, K2tog, yfwd, K3.
Row 10: P.
Rep these 10 rows.

EYELET MOCK cable (left section of picture)
CROSSED RIBS with faggotting (middle section of picture)
DIAMOND eyelet insertion (right section of picture)

Cables

Many knitters get addicted to cables, which quickly produce dramatic effects. Once you get used to working with a cable needle, you can easily change the position of groups of stitches to make the distinctive rope effect twist to the left or right. The same technique is used to create vertical panels, whether of simple cables or highly complex interlacing designs, and overall patterns.

Cable patterns are the main component of traditional Aran designs, which evolved on the Isles of Aran, west of Ireland, and resemble the interlaced patterns on Celtic crosses and stones. Traditional combinations are still very popular, but a single cable on an otherwise plain piece will also make a definite statement.

A background of Reverse Stockinette stitch—at least two purl stitches on each side of a panel—will enhance the definition of the cables. Interspersing complex patterns with a simple, regularly repeated cable or Basic Seed stitch panel is also very effective. Although traditionally worked in medium-weight plain, undyed wool, cables also show up well in bulky yarns or more subtly in fine or lightly textured yarns.

FOUR-STITCH cable (over 4 rows)
Panel of 4 sts on Reverse St st background
Row 1: (RS) K.
Row 2: P.
Row 3: C4F.
Row 4: P.
Rep these 4 rows.

SAND pattern
Multiples of 12 sts
Row 1: (RS) K.
Row 2 and all WS rows: P.
Row 3: *C6F, K6, rep from * to end.
Row 5: As row 1.
Row 7: *K6, C6B, rep from * to end.
Row 9: As row 1.
Row 10: P.
Rep rows 3–10.

FOUR-STITCH cable (over 6 rows)
Panel of 4 sts on Reverse St st background
Row 1: (RS) K.
Row 2 and all WS rows: P.
Row 3: As row 1.
Row 5: C4F.
Row 6: P.
Rep these 6 rows.

SIX-STITCH cable
(over 6 rows)
Panel of 6 sts on Reverse St st background
Rows 1 and 3: (RS) K.
Row 2 and all WS rows: P.
Row 5: C6F.
Row 6: P.
Rep these 6 rows.

TRELLIS cable
Panel of 30 sts on Reverse St st background
T5B = slip 2 sts onto CN and hold at back of work, K3, P2 from CN
T5F = slip 3 sts onto CN and hold at front of work, P2, K3 from CN
Rows 1, 3, and 5: (RS) (K3, P2) twice, K3, P4, K3, (P2, K3) twice.

Rows 2, 4, and 6: (P3, K2) twice, P3, K4, P3, (K2, P3) twice.
Row 7: T5F 3 times, T5B 3 times.
Row 8: (K2, P3) twice, K2, P6, K2, (P3, K2) twice.
Row 9: P2, T5F twice, C6B, T5B twice, P2.
Row 10: K4, P3, K2, P12, K2, P3, K4.
Row 11: P4, T5F, C6F twice, T5B, P4.
Row 12: K6, P18, K6.
Row 13: P6, C6B 3 times, P6.
Row 14: As row 12.
Row 15: P4, T5B, C6F twice, T5F, P4.
Row 16: As row 10.
Row 17: P2, T5B twice, C6B, T5F twice, P2.
Row 18: As row 8.

Row 19: T5B 3 times, T5F 3 times.
Rows 20 and 22: As row 2.
Rows 21 and 23: As row 1.
Row 24: As row 2.
Rep these 24 rows.

SIX-STITCH cable variation
Panel of 6 sts on Reverse St st background
Rows 1, 3, 7, 9, 13, and 15: (RS) K.
Row 2 and all WS rows: P.
Rows 5 and 11: C6F.
Row 16: P.
Rep these 16 rows.

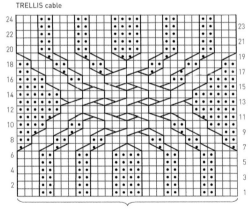

TRELLIS cable

30-stitch repeat

KEY

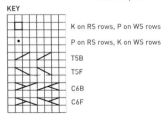

	K on RS rows, P on WS rows
•	P on RS rows, K on WS rows
	T5B
	T5F
	C6B
	C6F

SIX-STITCH cable (over 6 rows) (left section of picture)
TRELLIS cable (middle section of picture)
SIX-STITCH cable variation (right section of picture)

LOBSTER CLAW stitch

Panel of 8 sts on Reverse St st background

Row 1: (WS) K.

Row 2: K1, P6, K1.

Rows 3, 5, and 7: P2, K4, P2.

Rows 4 and 6: K2, P4, K2.

Row 8: sl2 onto CN and hold at front of work, P2, (yon, K2tog tbl) from CN, sl2 onto CN and hold at back of work, K2tog, (yrn, P2) from CN.

Rep these 8 rows.

CELTIC cable

Panel of 24 sts on Reverse St st background

T3B = slip 1 st onto CN and hold at back of work, K2, P1 from CN

T3F = slip 2 sts onto CN and hold at front of work, P1, K2 from CN

T4B = slip 2 sts onto CN and hold at back of work, K2, P2 from CN

T4F = slip 2 sts onto CN and hold at front of work, P2, K2 from CN

Row 1: (RS) (P2, C4B, P2) 3 times.

Row 2: (K2, P4, K2) 3 times.

Row 3: P1, T3B, (T4F, T4B) twice, T3F, P1.

Row 4: K1, P2, K3, P4, K4, P4, K3, P2, K1.

Row 5: T3B, P1, (P2, C4F, P2) twice, P1, T3F.

Row 6: P2, (K4, P4) twice, K4, P2.

Row 7: K2, P2, (T4B, T4F) twice, P2, K2.

Row 8: P2, K2, P2, K4, P4, K4, P2, K2, P2.

Row 9: (K2, P2) twice, P2, C4B, P2, (P2, K2) twice.

Row 10: As row 8.

Row 11: K2, P2, (T4F, T4B) twice, P2, K2.

Row 12: As row 6.

Row 13: T3F, P1, (P2, C4F, P2) twice, P1, T3B.

Row 14: As row 4.

Row 15: P1, T3F, (T4B, T4F) twice, T3B, P1.

Row 16: As row 2.

Rep these 16 rows.

DOUBLE cable (over 6 rows)

Panel of 7 sts on Reverse St st background

C3L = slip 1 st onto CN and hold at front of work, K2, K1 from CN

C3R = slip 2 sts onto CN and hold at back of work, K1, K2 from CN

Row 1: (RS) K.

Row 2: P.

Row 3: C3R, K1, C3L.

Row 4: P.

Rep these 4 rows.

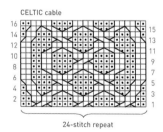

CELTIC cable

24-stitch repeat

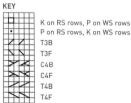

KEY

	K on RS rows, P on WS rows
•	P on RS rows, K on WS rows
	T3B
	T3F
	C4B
	C4F
	T4B
	T4F

LOBSTER CLAW stitch (left section of picture)

CELTIC cable (middle section of picture)

DOUBLE cable (over 6 rows) (right section of picture)

DOUBLE HONEYCOMB cable

Panel of 13 sts on Reverse St st background

Rows 1 and 3: (RS) K.
Row 2 and all WS rows: P.
Row 5: C6B, K1, C6F.
Rows 7, 9, and 11: K.
Row 13: C6F, K1, C6B.
Row 15: K.
Row 16: P.
Rep these 16 rows.

MOSS DIAMOND cable

Panel of 17 sts on Reverse St st background

Cr5B = slip 3 sts onto CN and hold at back of work, K2, slip P st onto LHN and P it, K2 from CN
T3B = slip 1 st onto CN and hold at back of work, K2, P1 from CN
T3F = slip 2 sts onto CN and hold at front of work, P1, K2 from CN
Row 1: (RS) P6, K2, P1, K2, P6.
Row 2: K6, P2, K1, P2, K6.
Row 3: P6, Cr5B, P6.
Row 4: As row 2.
Row 5: P5, T3B, K1, T3F, P5.
Row 6: K5, P2, K1, P1, K1, P2, K5.
Row 7: P4, T3B, K1, P1, K1, T3F, P4.
Row 8: K4, P2, (K1, P1) twice, K1, P2, K4.
Row 9: P3, T3B, (K1, P1) twice, K1, T3F, P3.
Row 10: K3, P2, (K1, P1) 3 times, K1, P2, K3.
Row 11: P2, T3B, (K1, P1) 3 times, K1, T3F, P2.
Row 12: K2, P2, (K1, P1) 4 times, K1, P2, K2.
Row 13: P2, T3F, (P1, K1) 3 times, P1, T3B, P2.
Row 14: As row 10.
Row 15: P3, T3F, (P1, K1) twice, P1, T3B, P3.
Row 16: As row 8.
Row 17: P4, T3F, P1, K1, P1, T3B, P4.
Row 18: As row 6.
Row 19: P5, T3F, P1, T3B, P5.
Row 20: As row 2.
Rep these 20 rows.

ASYMMETRIC cable

Panel of 6 sts on Reverse St st background

Rows 1 and 5: (RS) K2, C4F.
Row 2 and all WS rows: P.
Row 3: K.
Rows 7 and 11: C4B, K2.
Row 9: K.
Row 12: P.
Rep these 12 rows.

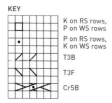

MOSS DIAMOND cable

17-stitch repeat

KEY

K on RS rows, P on WS rows

P on RS rows, K on WS rows

T3B

T3F

Cr5B

DOUBLE HONEYCOMB cable (left section of picture)
MOSS DIAMOND cable (middle section of picture)
ASYMMETRIC cable (right section of picture)

CROSSED CABLE pattern

Multiples of 8 sts plus 6

Rows 1 and all WS rows: *K2, P2, rep from * to last 2 sts, K2.

Rows 2, 4, and 6: *P2, K2, rep from * to last 2 sts, P2.

Row 8: *P2, C6F, rep from * to last 6 sts, P2, K2, P2.

Rows 10, 12, and 14: *P2, K2, rep from * to last 2 sts, P2.

Row 16: P2, K2, P2, *C6B, P2, rep from * to end.

Rep these 16 rows.

LINK cable

Panel of 8 sts on Reverse St st background

Rows 1, 3, 5, and 7: (WS) P.

Row 2: C4B, C4F.

Rows 4, 6, and 8: K.

Rep these 8 rows.

MEDALLION panel

Panel of 8 sts on Reverse St st background

Rows 1 and 3: (RS) K.

Row 2: P.

Row 4: yfwd, sl1, P6, sl1.

Row 5: slip 1 st onto CN and hold at front of work, P3, K1 from CN, slip 3 sts onto CN and hold at back of work, K1, P3 from CN.

Row 6: K3, P2, K3.

Row 7: slip 3 sts onto CN and hold at back of work, K1, K3 from CN, slip 1 st onto CN and hold at front of work, K3, K1 from CN.

Row 8: P.

Rep these 8 rows.

CROSSED CABLE pattern (left section of picture)

LINK cable (middle section of picture)

MEDALLION panel (right section of picture)

WAVY cable

Panel of 4 sts on Reverse St st background

Rows 1, 3, 7, and 9: (RS) K.
Row 2 and all WS rows: P.
Row 5: C4B.
Row 11: C4F.
Row 12: P.
Rep these 12 rows.

CABLE AND FAN pattern

Panel of 19 sts on Reverse St st background

C7B = slip 4 sts onto CN and hold at back of work, K3, K4 from CN

Row 1: (RS) P6, K7, P6.
Row 2: K6, P7, K6.
Row 3: P6, C7B, P6.
Row 4: As row 2.
Row 5: P4, K3tog, yfwd, K1, yfwd, K2tog, (yfwd, K1) twice, yfwd, K3tog tbl, P4.
Row 6: K4, P11, K4.
Row 7: P3, (K2tog, yfwd) 3 times, K1 tbl, (yfwd, SKP) 3 times, P3.
Row 8: K3, P13, K3.
Row 9: P1, K3tog, (yfwd, K2tog) twice, yfwd, K1 tbl, yfwd, K1, yfwd, K1 tbl, (yfwd, SKP) twice, yfwd, K3tog tbl, P1.
Row 10: K1, P17, K1.
Row 11: P2, (K2tog, yfwd) 3 times, K1 tbl, K1, K1 tbl, (yfwd, SKP) 3 times, P2.
Row 12: K2, P15, K2.
Row 13: P3, (K2tog, yfwd) twice, K1 tbl, K3, K1 tbl, (yfwd, SKP) twice, P3.
Row 14: As row 8.
Row 15: P4, K2tog, yfwd, K1 tbl, K5, K1 tbl, yfwd, SKP, P4.
Row 16: As row 6.
Row 17: As row 1.
Row 18: As row 2.
Row 19: As row 3.
Row 20: As row 2.
Rows 21, 23, and 25: As row 1.
Rows 22, 24, and 26: As row 2.
Row 27: As row 3.
Row 28: As row 2.
Rows 29 and 31: As row 1.
Rows 30 and 32: As row 2.
Rep these 32 rows.

HONEYCOMB CABLE pattern

Panel of 8 sts on Reverse St st background

Rows 1 and 5: (RS) K.
Row 2 and all WS rows: P.
Row 3: C4F, C4B.
Row 7: C4B, C4F.
Row 8: P.
Rep these 8 rows.

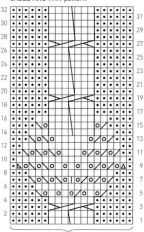

CABLE AND FAN pattern

19-stitch repeat

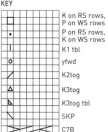

KEY

□	K on RS rows, P on WS rows
•	P on RS rows, K on WS rows
ǀ	K1 tbl
o	yfwd
╱	K2tog
△	K3tog
◣	K3tog tbl
╲	SKP
╳	C7B

WAVY cable (left section of picture)
CABLE AND FAN pattern (middle section of picture)
HONEYCOMB CABLE pattern (right section of picture)

TWISTED PATH cable

Panel of 17 sts on Reverse St st background

B3 = (bind 3) sl1k, K1, yfwd, K1, psso (K1, yfwd, K1)

T4L = slip 3 sts onto CN and hold at front of work, P1, K3 from CN

T4R = slip 1 st onto CN and hold at back of work, K3, P1 from CN

T5B = slip 2 sts onto CN and hold at back of work, K3, P2 from CN

T5F = slip 3 sts onto CN and hold at front of work, P2, K3 from CN

Row 1: (RS) P1, T4L, T5B, P3, T4L.

Row 2: P3, K6, P6, K2.

Row 3: P2, C6B, P6, B3.

Row 4: As row 2.

Rows 5 and 7: P2, K6, P6, B3.

Rows 6 and 8: As row 2.

Row 9: As row 3.

Row 10: As row 2.

Row 11: P1, T4R, T5F, P3, T4R.

Row 12: K1, P3, (K3, P3) twice, K1.

Row 13: T4R, P3, T5F, T4R, P1.

Row 14: K2, P6, K6, P3.

Row 15: B3, P6, C6F, P2.

Row 16: As row 14.

Rows 17 and 19: B3, P6, K6, P2.

Rows 18 and 20: As row 14.

Row 21: As row 15.

Row 22: As row 14.

Row 23: T4L, P3, T5B, T4L, P1.

Row 24: As row 12.

Rep these 24 rows.

WILD OATS pattern

Multiples of 4 sts plus 1

Rows 1 and 5: (RS) *K2, sl1, K1, rep from * to last st, K1.

Rows 2 and 6: P1, *P1, sl1, P2, rep from * to end.

Row 3: *slip next 2 sts onto CN and hold at back of work, K the slip st on LHN, K2 from CN, K1, rep from * to last st, K1.

Row 4: P.

Row 7: K1, *K1, slip the slip st onto CN and hold at front of work, K2, K1 from CN, rep from * to end.

Row 8: P.

Rep these 8 rows.

TIED cable

Multiples of 10 sts plus 2

Rows 1 and 3: (RS) K1, *P1, K4, P2, K2, P1, rep from * to last st, K1.

Rows 2, 4, 6, and 8: P1, *K1, P2, K2, P4, K1, rep from * to last st, P1.

Row 5: K1, *P1, C4B, P2, K2, P1, rep from * to last st, K1.

Row 7: As row 1.

Rows 9 and 11: K1, *P2, K2, P2, K4, rep from * to last st, K1.

Rows 10, 12, and 14: P1 *P4, K2, P2, K2, rep from * to last st, P1.

Row 13: K1, * P2, K2, P2, C4B, rep from * to last st, K1.

Row 15: As row 9.

Row 16: As row 10.

Rep these 16 rows.

TWISTED PATH cable (left section of picture)

WILD OATS pattern (middle section of picture)

TIED cable (right section of picture)

MEDALLION AND ANTLER cable

Panel of 6 sts on Reverse St st background

C3L = slip 1 st onto CN and hold at front of work, K2, K1 from CN
C3R = slip 2 sts onto CN and hold at back of work, K1, K2 from CN
Rows 1, 3, and 11: (RS) K.
Row 2 and all WS rows: P.
Rows 5, 7, and 9: C3R, C3L.
Row 12: P.
Rep these 12 rows.

RIBBED cable

Panel of 7 sts on Reverse St st background

Cr7B rib = slip 4 sts onto CN and hold at front of work, (K1, P1, K1) from LHN, slip 4th st from CN to LHN and P, (K1, P1, K1) from CN
Rows 1, 3, and 5: (RS) K1 tbl, (P1 tbl, K1 tbl) 3 times.
Row 2 and all WS rows: P1 tbl, (K1 tbl, P1 tbl) 3 times.
Row 7: Cr7B rib.
Rows 9, 11, 13, and 15: As row 1.
Row 16: As row 2.
Rep these 16 rows.

PATCHWORK cable

Panel of 15 sts on Reverse St st background

T3R = slip 1 st onto CN and hold at back of work, K2, P1 from CN
T3F = slip 2 sts onto CN and hold at front of work, P1, K2 from CN
T4B = slip 2 sts onto CN and hold at back of work, K2, P2 from CN
T4F = slip 2 sts onto CN and hold at front of work, P2, K2 from CN
Row 1: (RS) K2, (K1, P1) 3 times, K5, P2.
Row 2: K2, P4, (K1, P1) 3 times, K1, P2.
Row 3: T3F, (P1, K1) 3 times, C4F, P2.
Row 4: K2, P4, (K1, P1) 3 times, P2, K1.
Row 5: P1, T3F, K1, P1, K1, T4B, C3F, P1.
Row 6: K1, P2, P1 tbl, K1, P1 tbl, P2, K1, P1, K1, P2, K2.
Row 7: P2, T3F, T4B, K1 tbl, P1, K1 tbl, T3F.

Row 8: P2, (K1, P1 tbl) 3 times, P4, K3.
Row 9: P3, T4B, (K1 tbl, P1) 3 times, K2.
Row 10: P2, (K1, P1 tbl) 4 times, P2, K3.
Row 11: P1, T4B, (K1 tbl, P1) 3 times, K1 tbl, T3B.
Row 12: K1, P2, (P1 tbl, K1) 4 times, P1 tbl, P2, K1.
Row 13: T3B, (K1 tbl, P1) 3 times, K1 tbl, T4B, P1.
Row 14: K3, P2, (P1 tbl, K1) 4 times, P2.
Row 15: K2, (P1, K1 tbl) 3 times, C4B, P3.
Row 16: K3, P4, (P1, K1 tbl) 3 times, P2.
Row 17: T3F, K1 tbl, P1, K1 tbl, T4B, C3F, P2.
Row 18: K2, P2, K1, P1, K1, P2, P1 tbl, K1, P1 tbl, P2, K1.
Row 19: P1, T3F, T4B, K1, P1, K1, T3F, P1.
Row 20: K1, P2, (P1, K1) 3 times, P4, K2.
Row 21: P2, C4F, (K1, P1) 3 times, C3F.
Row 22: P2, (K1, P1) 3 times, K1, P4, K2.
Row 23: P2, K4, (K1, P1) 3 times, K3.
Row 24: As row 22.
Row 25: P2, C4F, (K1, P1) 3 times, T3B.
Row 26: As row 20.
Row 27: P1, C3B, T4F, K1, P1, K1, T3B, P1.
Row 28: As row 18.
Row 29: T3B, K1 tbl, P1, K1 tbl, T4F, T3B, P2.
Row 30: As row 16.
Row 31: K2, (P1, K1 tbl) 3 times, T4F, P3.
Row 32: As row 14.
Row 33: T3F, (K1 tbl, P1) 3 times, K1 tbl, T4F, P1.
Row 34: As row 12.
Row 35: P1, T4F, (K1 tbl, P1) 3 times, K1 tbl, T3F.
Row 36: As row 10.
Row 37: P3, C4F, (K1 tbl, P1) 3 times, K2.
Row 38: As row 8.

Row 39: P2, C3B, T4F, K1 tbl, P1, K1 tbl, T3B.
Row 40: As row 6.
Row 41: P1, T3B, K1, P1, K1, T4F, T3B, P1.
Row 42: As row 4.
Row 43: C3B, (P1, K1) 3 times, C4F, P2.
Row 44: As row 2.
Rep these 44 rows.

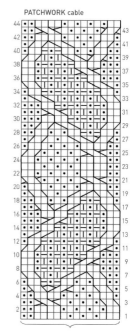

PATCHWORK cable

15-stitch repeat

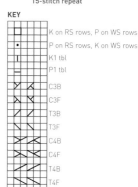

KEY

K on RS rows, P on WS rows
P on RS rows, K on WS rows
K1 tbl
P1 tbl
C3B
C3F
T3B
T3F
C4B
C4F
T4B
T4F

MEDALLION AND ANTLER cable
(outer sections of picture)
RIBBED cable (inner sections of picture)
PATCHWORK cable (central section of picture)

FIVE-RIB braid

Panel of 14 sts on Reverse St st background

Cr5B = slip 3 sts onto CN and hold at back of work, K2, slip P st onto LHN and P it, K2 from CN

Cr5F = slip 3 sts onto CN and hold at front of work, K2, slip P st onto LHN and P it, K2 from CN

Row 1: (RS) (K2, P1) 4 times, K2.

Row 2 and all WS rows: (P2, K1) 4 times, P2.

Row 3: K2, (P1, Cr5F) twice.

Row 5: As row 1.

Row 7: (Cr5B, P1) twice, K2.

Row 8: As row 2.

Rep these 8 rows.

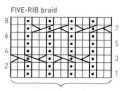

FIVE-RIB braid

14-stitch repeat

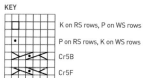

KEY

□	K on RS rows, P on WS rows
•	P on RS rows, K on WS rows
⤬	Cr5B
⤬	Cr5F

OPEN ROPE cable

Panel of 16 sts on Reverse St st background

T3B = slip 1 st onto CN and hold at back of work, K2, P1 from CN

T3F = slip 2 sts onto CN and hold at front of work, P1, K2 from CN

Row 1: (RS) K2, P4, K4, P4, K2.

Row 2: P2, K4, P4, K4, P2.

Row 3: K2, P4, C4B, P4, K2.

Row 4: As row 2.

Row 5: (T3F, P2, T3B) twice.

Row 6: K1, P2, (K2, P2) 3 times, K1.

Row 7: P1, T3F, T3B, P2, T3F, T3B, P1.

Row 8: K2, P4, K4, P4, K2.

Row 9: P2, C4B, P4, C4B, P2.

Row 10: As row 8.

Row 11: As row 2.

Row 12: As row 8.

Row 13: As row 9.

Row 14: As row 8.

Row 15: P1, T3B, T3F, P2, T3B, T3F, P1.

Row 16: As row 6.

Row 17: (T3B, P2, T3F) twice.

Row 18: As row 2.

Row 19: As row 3.

Row 20: As row 2.

Rep these 20 rows.

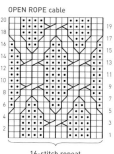

OPEN ROPE cable

16-stitch repeat

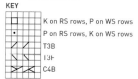

KEY

□	K on RS rows, P on WS rows
•	P on RS rows, K on WS rows
╱	T3B
╲	T3F
⤬	C4B

FOUR-RIB braid

Panel of 13 sts on Reverse St st background

Cr5F = slip 3 st onto CN and hold at front of work, K2, slip P st onto LHN and P it, K2 from CN

T3B = slip 1 st onto CN and hold at back of work, K2, P1 from CN

T3F = slip 2 sts onto CN and hold at front of work, P1, K2 from CN

Row 1: (WS) P2, K2, P2, K1, P2, K2, P2.

Row 2: K2, P2, Cr5F, P2, K2.

Row 3: As row 1.

Row 4: T3F, T3B, P1, T3F, T3B.

Row 5: K1, P4, K3, P4, K1.

Row 6: P1, C4B, P3, C4F, P1.

Row 7: As row 5.

Row 8: T3B, T3F, P1, T3B, T3F.

Rep these 8 rows.

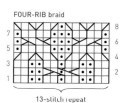

FOUR-RIB braid

13-stitch repeat

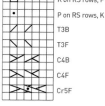

KEY

□	K on RS rows, P on WS rows
•	P on RS rows, K on WS rows
╱	T3B
╲	T3F
⤬	C4B
⤬	C4F
⤬	Cr5F

FIVE-RIB braid (left section of picture)

OPEN ROPE cable (middle section of picture)

FOUR-RIB braid (right section of picture)

TWISTED cable

Panel of 8 sts on Reverse St st background

Row 1: (WS) P.
Row 2: (C4B) twice.
Row 3: P.
Row 4: K2, C4B, K2.
Rep these 4 rows.

SEEDED cable

Panel of 8 sts on Reverse St st background

Rows 1 and 3: (RS) K4, (K1, P1) twice.
Rows 2 and 4: (P1, K1) twice, P4.
Row 5: Slip 4 sts onto CN and hold at back of work, (K1, P1) twice from LHN, K4 from CN.
Rows 6, 8, 10, and 12: P4 (P1, K1) twice.
Rows 7, 9, and 11: (K1, P1) twice, K4.
Row 13: Slip 4 sts onto CN and hold at back of work, K4 from LHN, (K1, P1) twice from CN.
Row 14: As row 2.
Row 15: As row 1.
Row 16: As row 2.
Rep these 16 rows.

STRANDED cable

Panel of 16 sts on Reverse St st background

Row 1: (RS) K1, P2, (K2, P2) 3 times, K1.
Row 2: P1, K2, (P2, K2) 3 times, P1.
Row 3: Slip 4 sts onto CN and hold at back of work, K1, P2, K1 from LH needle, K1, P2, K1 from CN, slip 4 sts onto CN and hold at front of work, K1, P2, K1 from LH needle, K1, P2, K1 from CN.
Row 4: (P1, K2, P1) 4 times.
Rows 5, 7, 9, 11, and 13: As row 1.
Rows 6, 8, 10, 12, and 14: As row 2.
Row 15: Slip 4 sts onto CN and hold at front of work, K1, P2, K1 from LH needle, K1, P2, K1 from CN, slip 4 sts onto CN and hold at back of work, K1, P2, K1 from LH needle, K1, P2, K1 from CN.
Row 16: As row 4.
Rows 17, 19, 21, and 23: As row 1.
Rows 18, 20, 22, and 24: As row 2.
Rep these 24 rows.

TWISTED cable (outer sections of picture)
SEEDED cable (inner sections of picture)
STRANDED cable (central section of picture)

OXO cable

Panel of 8 sts on Reverse St st background

Row 1: (RS) K.
Row 2: P.
Row 3: C4B, C4F.
Row 4: P.
Rows 5–8: As rows 1–4.
Row 9: K.
Row 10: P.
Row 11: C4F, C4B.
Row 12: P.
Rows 13–16: As rows 9–12.
Rep these 16 rows.

BRAID cable

Panel of 9 sts on Reverse St st background

T3B = slip 1 st onto CN and hold at back of work, K2, P1 from CN
T3F = slip 2 sts onto CN and hold at front of work, P1, K2 from CN
Row 1: (RS) T3F, T3B, T3F.
Row 2: P2, K2, P4, K1.
Row 3: P1, C4B, P2, K2.
Row 4: P2, K2, P4, K1.
Row 5: T3B, T3F, T3B.
Row 6: K1, P4, K2, P2.
Row 7: K2, P2, C4F, P1.
Row 8: K1, P4, K2, P2.
Rep these 8 rows.

ANTLER cable

Panel of 16 sts on Reverse St st background

Row 1 and all WS rows: P.
Row 2: K4, C4B, C4F, K4.
Row 4: K2, C4B, K4, C4F, K2.
Row 6: C4B, K8, C4F.
Rep these 6 rows.

LATTICE stitch

Multiples of 4 sts plus 2

Row 1: (RS) K2, *C4F, rep from
* to end.

Row 2: P.

Row 3: *C4B, rep from * to last
2 sts, K2.

Row 4: P.

Rep these 4 rows.

TWISTED CELTIC cable

Panel of 20 sts on Reverse St st
background

T3B = slip 1 st onto CN and
hold at back, K2, P1 from CN

T3F = slip 2 sts onto CN and
hold at front, P1, K2 from CN

Row 1: (RS) P4, C4B, P4, C4F,
P4.

Row 2: K4, (P4, K4) twice.

Row 3: P3, T3B, T3F, P2, T3B,
T3F, P3.

Row 4: K3, (P2, K2) 3 times,
P2, K3.

Row 5: P2, (T3B, P2, T3F)
twice, P2.

Row 6: K2, P2, K4, P4, K4,
P2, K2.

Row 7: P2, K2, P4, C4B, P4,
K2, P2.

Row 8: K2, P2, K4, P4, K4,
P2, K2.

Row 9: P2, K2, P4, K4, P4,
K2, P2.

Row 10: As row 8.

Row 11: As row 7.

Row 12: As row 8.

Row 13: P2, (T3F, P2, T3B)
twice, P2.

Row 14: As row 4.

Row 15: P3, T3F, T3B, P2, T3F,
T3B, P3.

Row 16: As row 2.

Row 17: As row 1.

Row 18: As row 2.

Row 19: As row 3.

Row 20: As row 4.

Row 21: P3, (K2, P2) twice, K2,
slip last 6 sts onto CN, wrap
yarn around them 4 times
counterclockwise and slip them
back onto RHN, P2, K2, P3.

Row 22: As row 4.

Row 23: As row 15.

Row 24: As row 2.

Rep these 24 rows.

OPEN LATTICE stitch

Multiples of 6 sts plus 2

T4B = slip 2 sts onto CN and
hold at back of work, K2, P2
from CN

T4F = slip 2 sts onto CN and
hold at front of work, P2, K2
from CN

Row 1: (WS) K3, P4, *K2, P4,
rep from * to last st, K1.

Row 2: P1, C4F, *P2, C4F, rep
from * to last 3 sts, P3.

Row 3: As row 1.

Row 4: P3, *K2, T4B, rep from *
to last 5 sts, K4, P1.

Row 5: K1, P4, *K2, P4, rep
from * to last 3 sts, K3.

Row 6: P3, C4B, *P2, C4B, rep
from * to last st, P1.

Row 7: As row 5.

Row 8: P1, K4, *T4F, K2, rep
from * to last 3 sts, P3.

Rep these 8 rows.

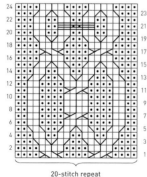

TWISTED CELTIC cable

24 22 20 18 16 14 12 10 8 6 4 2

23 21 19 17 15 13 11 9 7 5 3 1

20-stitch repeat

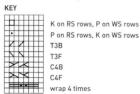

KEY

K on RS rows, P on WS rows
P on RS rows, K on WS rows
T3B
T3F
C4B
C4F
wrap 4 times

LATTICE stitch (left section of picture)
TWISTED CELTIC cable (middle section of picture)
OPEN LATTICE stitch (right section of picture)

184 cables

Knitted lace

This section presents a wide variety of lacy patterns, from gossamer Shetland lace to meshes such as Eyelet stitch and the ornamental effects of twisted eyelets. They all have a high proportion of openwork background and look best when the patterns are stretched to open them out. Most of the stitch patterns here have been shown in a plain medium-weight cashmere, which shows off the lace well; but one or two with a strong Shetland connection have been worked in fine Shetland wool to give a taste of the finer effects that can be achieved.

Although Shetland lace was traditionally knitted in the wonderfully soft cobweb-weight wool of the islands' sheep, a lace-weight yarn worked on size 2 (2.75 mm) needles is less difficult and will produce truly beautiful results in patterns such as Horseshoe, Falling Leaves, Feather and Fan, or Diamond lace. Especially on finer pieces, keep your casting on flexible and inconspicuous by using the single cast-on method described on page 20.

Many of the stitch patterns have evocative names: imagine Print o' the Wave, Candlelight, or Spanish lace being passed down from one generation of knitters to another.

SPANISH lace
Multiples of 34 sts plus 2

Row 1: (RS) K1, *K3, K2tog, K4, yfrn, P2, (K2, yfwd, SKP) 3 times, P2, yon, K4, SKP, K3, rep from * to last st, K1.

Row 2: K1, *P2, P2tog tbl, P4, yrn, P1, K2, (P2, yrn, P2tog) 3 times, K2, P1, yrn, P4, P2tog, P2, rep from * to last st, K1.

Row 3: K1, *K1, K2tog, K4, yfwd, K2, P2, (K2, yfwd, SKP) 3 times, P2, K2, yfwd, K4, SKP, K1, rep from * to last st, K1.

Row 4: K1, *P2tog tbl, P4, yrn, P3, K2, (P2, yrn, P2tog) 3 times, K2, P3, yrn, P4, P2tog, rep from * to last st, K1.

Rows 5–12: Rep rows 1–4 twice more.

Row 13: K1, *yfwd, SKP, K2, yfwd, SKP, P2, yon, K4, SKP, K6, K2tog, K4, yfrn, P2, K2, yfwd, SKP, K2, rep from * to last st, K1.

Row 14: K1, *yon, P2tog, P2, yrn, P2tog, K2, P1, yrn, P4, P2tog, P4, P2tog tbl, P4, yrn, P1, K2, P2, yrn, P2tog, P2, rep from * to last st, K1.

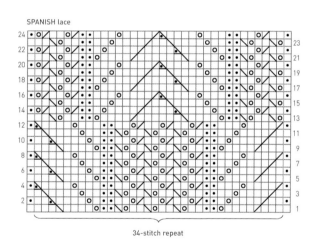

34-stitch repeat

Row 15: K1, *yfwd, SKP, K2, yfwd, SKP, P2, K2, yfwd, K4, SKP, K2, K2tog, K4, yfwd, K2, P2, K2, yfwd, SKP, K2, rep from * to last st, K1.

Row 16: K1, *yfrn, P2tog, P2, yrn, P2tog, K2, P3, yon, P4, P2tog, P2tog tbl, P4, yrn, P3, K2, P2, yrn, P2tog, P2, rep from * to last st, K1.

Rows 17–24: Rep rows 13–16 twice more.
Rep these 24 rows.

KEY

☐	K on RS rows, P on WS rows
•	P on RS rows, K on WS rows
O	yfwd, yrn or yfrn
╱	K2tog tbl
◣	P2tog on WS rows
╲	SKP
	start and end of the repeat

SPANISH lace

ALTERNATING FEATHER stitch

Multiples of 6 sts plus 1

Rows 1, 3, 5, 7, 9, and 11: (RS) *K1, K2tog, yfwd, K1, yfwd, SKP, rep from * to last st, K1.

Rows 2 and all WS rows: P.

Rows 13, 15, 17, 19, 21, and 23: *K1, yfwd, SKP, K1, K2tog, yfwd, rep from * to last st, K1.

Row 24: P.

Rep these 24 rows.

SIMPLE lace

Multiples of 6 sts plus 1

Row 1 and all WS rows: P.

Rows 2, 4, and 6: K1, *yfwd, SKP, K1, K2tog, yfwd, K1, rep from * to end.

Row 8: K2, *yfwd, SK2P, yfwd, K3, rep from *, ending last rep K2.

Row 10: K1, *K2tog, yfwd, K1, yfwd, SKP, K1, rep from * to end.

Row 12: K2tog, *yfwd, K3, yfwd, SK2P, rep from *, ending last rep SKP.

Rep these 12 rows.

TRAVELING FERN pattern

Multiples of 16 sts

Row 1: (RS) *K9, yfwd, K1, yfwd, K3, SK2P, rep from * to end.

Row 2 and all WS rows: P.

Row 3: *K10, yfwd, K1, yfwd, K2, SK2P, rep from * to end.

Row 5: *K3tog, K4, yfwd, K1, yfwd, K3, (yfwd, K1) twice, SK2P, rep from * to end.

Row 7: *K3tog, K3, yfwd, K1, yfwd, K9, rep from * to end.

Row 9: *K3tog, K2, yfwd, K1, yfwd, K10, rep from * to end.

Row 11: *K3tog, (K1, yfwd) twice, K3, yfwd, K1, yfwd, K4, SK2P, rep from * to end.

Row 12: P.

Rep these 12 rows.

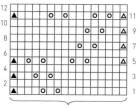

TRAVELING FERN pattern

16-stitch repeat

KEY

	K on RS rows, P on WS rows
O	yfwd
△	K3tog
▲	SK2P

ALTERNATING FEATHER stitch (top section of picture)
SIMPLE lace (middle section of picture)
TRAVELING FERN pattern (bottom section of picture)

CAT'S EYE net (reversible)

Multiples of 4 sts

Row 1: (RS) P2, *yrn, P4tog, rep from * to last 2 sts, P2.

Row 2: K2, *K1, (K1, P1, K1) into yrn on previous row, rep from * to last 2 sts, K2.

Row 3: K.

Rep these 3 rows.

CANDLELIGHT lace

Multiples of 10 sts plus 11

Row 1: (RS) *K3, K2tog, yfwd, K1, yfwd, SKP, K2, rep from * to last st, K1.

Row 2 and all WS rows: P.

Row 3: *K2, K2tog, (K1, yfwd) twice, K1, SKP, K1, rep from * to last st, K1.

Row 5: *K1, K2tog, K2, yfwd, K1, yfwd, K2, SKP, rep from * to last st, K1.

Row 7: K2tog, K3, yfwd, K1, yfwd, K3, * SK2P, K3, yfwd, K1, yfwd, K3, rep from * to last 2 sts, SKP.

Row 9: *K1, yfwd, SKP, K5, K2tog, yfwd, rep from * to last st, K1.

Row 11: *K1, yfwd, K1, SKP, K3, K2tog, K1, yfwd, rep from * to last st, K1.

Row 13: *K1, yfwd, K2, SKP, K2tog, K2, yfwd, rep from * to last st, K1.

Row 15: *K1, yfwd, K3, SK2P, K3, yfwd, rep from * to last st, K1.

Row 16: P.

Rep these 16 rows.

LAMB'S LETTUCE lace

Multiples of 10 sts plus 1

Row 1: (RS) K2tog, *yfwd, K3, yfwd, inc1 K, yfwd, K3, yfwd, SK2P, rep from *, ending last rep SKP.

Row 2 and all WS rows: P.

Row 3: K2tog, *yfwd, K3tog, yfwd, K2tog, yfwd, SKP, yfwd, sl2, K1, p2sso, yfwd, SK2P, rep from *, ending last rep SKP.

Row 5: K3, *K2tog, yfwd, K1, yfwd, SKP, K5, rep from *, ending last rep K3.

Row 7: K2, *K2tog, yfwd, K3, yfwd, SKP, K3, rep from *, ending last rep K2.

Row 9: K3tog, * yfwd, K1, yfwd, K3, yfwd, K1, yfwd, sl2, K1, p2sso, slip last st from RHN to LHN and pass next 2 sts over it, slip it back onto RHN, rep from * to last 8 sts, yfwd, K1, yfwd, K3, yfwd, K1, yfwd, sl2, K1, p2sso.

Row 11: K1, *K2tog, yfwd, K1, yfwd, SK2P, yfwd, K1, yfwd, SKP, K1, rep from * to end.

Row 12: P.

Rep these 12 rows.

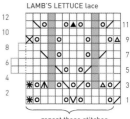

LAMB'S LETTUCE lace

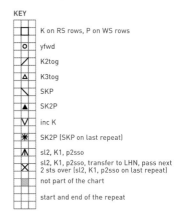

repeat these stitches

KEY

☐	K on RS rows, P on WS rows
o	yfwd
/	K2tog
△	K3tog
\	SKP
▲	SK2P
V	inc K
✱	SK2P (SKP on last repeat)
⋀	sl2, K1, p2sso
⊠	sl2, K1, p2sso, transfer to LHN, pass next 2 sts over (sl2, K1, p2sso on last repeat)
▓	not part of the chart
	start and end of the repeat

CANDLELIGHT lace

10-stitch repeat

KEY

☐	K on RS rows, P on WS rows
o	yfwd
/	K2tog
\	SKP
▲	SK2P
	start and end of the repeat

TURKISH stitch
Multiples of 2 sts (reversible)
All rows: K1, *yrn, SKP, rep from * to last st, K1.

TRAILING LEAVES pattern
Multiples of 15 sts plus 1
Row 1: (RS) *K1, yfwd, K1, SKP, P1, K2tog, K1, yfrn, P1, ybk, SKP, P1, K2tog, yfwd, K1, yfwd, rep from * to last st, K1.
Row 2: P1, *P4, K1, P1, K1, P3, K1, P4, rep from * to end.
Row 3: *K1, yfwd, K1, SKP, P1, K2tog, K1, P1, ybk, SK2P, yfwd, K3, yfwd, rep from * to last st, K1.
Row 4: P1, *P6, K1, P2, K1, P4, rep from * to end.
Row 5: *(K1, yfwd) twice, SKP, P1, K2tog twice, yfwd, K5, yfwd, rep from * to last st, K1.
Row 6: P1, *P7, K1, P1, K1, P5, rep from * to end.
Row 7: *K1, yfwd, K3, yfwd, SK2P, P1, yfwd, K1, SKP, P1, K2tog, K1, yfwd, rep from * to last st, K1.
Row 8: P1, *(P3, K1) twice, P7, rep from * to end.
Row 9: *K1, yfwd, K5, yfwd, K2tog tbl, K1, SKP, P1, K2tog, K1, yfwd, rep from * to last st, K1.
Row 10: P1, *P3, K1, P2, K1, P8, rep from * to end.
Rep these 10 rows.

FALLING LEAVES lace
Multiples of 10 sts plus 1
Row 1: (RS) K1, *yfwd, K3, SK2P, K3, yfwd, K1, rep from * to end.
Row 2 and all WS rows: P.
Row 3: K1, *K1, yfwd, K2, SK2P, K2, yfwd, K2, rep from * to end.
Row 5: K1, *K2, yfwd, K1, SK2P, K1, yfwd, K3, rep from * to end.
Row 7: K1, *K3, yfwd, SK2P, yfwd, K4, rep from * to end.
Row 9: K2tog, *K3, yfwd, K1, yfwd, K3, SK2P, rep from *, ending last rep SKP.
Row 11: K2tog, *K2, yfwd, K3, yfwd, K2, SK2P, rep from *, ending last rep SKP.
Row 13: K2tog, *K1, yfwd, K5, yfwd, K1, SK2P, rep from *, ending last rep SKP.
Row 15: K2tog, *yfwd, K7, yfwd, SK2P, rep from *, ending last rep SKP.
Row 16: P.
Rep these 16 rows.

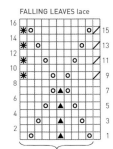

FALLING LEAVES lace

10-stitch repeat

KEY

	K on RS rows, P on WS rows
o	yfwd
/	K2tog
▲	SKP
✳	SK2P
	start and end of the repeat

TRAILING LEAVES pattern

15-stitch repeat

KEY

	K on RS rows, P on WS rows
•	P on RS rows, K on WS rows
o	yfwd
/	K2tog
\	K2tog tbl
▲	SKP
▲	SK2P
	not part of the chart
	start and end of the repeat

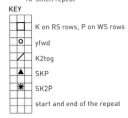

TURKISH stitch (top section of picture)
TRAILING LEAVES pattern (middle section of picture)
FALLING LEAVES lace (bottom section of picture)

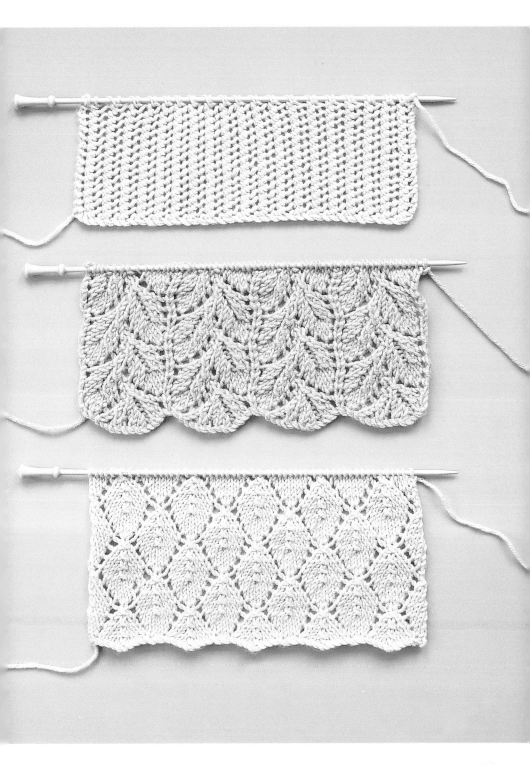

CELL stitch

Multiples of 4 sts plus 3
Row 1: (RS) K2, *yfwd, SK2P, yfwd, K1, rep from * to last st, K1.
Row 2: P.
Row 3: K1, K2tog, yfwd, K1, *yfwd, SK2P, yfwd, K1, rep from * to last 3 sts, yfwd, SKP, K1.
Row 4: P.
Rep these 4 rows.

DIAMOND EYELET pattern

Multiples of 6 sts plus 1
Row 1: (RS) P1, *K5, P1, rep from * to end.
Row 2: K1, *P5, K1, rep from * to end.
Row 3: P1, *yon, SKP, K1, K2tog, yfrn, P1, rep from * to end.
Row 4: K1, *K1 tbl, P3, K1 tbl, K1, rep from * to end.
Row 5: P2, *yon, sl1, K2, psso the K2, yfrn, P3, rep from *, ending last rep P2.
Row 6: K2, *K1 tbl, P1, K1 tbl, K3, rep from *, ending last rep K2.
Row 7: P2, *K2tog, yfwd, SKP, P3, rep from *, ending last rep P2.
Row 8: K1, *P2tog tbl, yrn, P1, yrn, P2tog, K1, rep from * to end.
Rep these 8 rows.

APPLE LEAVES lace

Multiples of 19 sts plus 2
Rows 1 and 3: (RS) K1, *SKP, K3, (yfwd, SKP) twice, yfwd, K1, yfwd, (K2tog, yfwd) twice, K3, K2tog, rep from * to last st, K1.
Row 2 and all WS rows: P.
Row 5: K1, *SKP, K2, (yfwd, K2tog) twice, yfwd, K3, yfwd, (SKP, yfwd) twice, K2, K2tog, rep from * to last st, K1.
Row 7: K1, *SKP, K1, (yfwd, K2tog) twice, yfwd, K5, yfwd, (SKP, yfwd) twice, K1, K2tog, rep from * to last st, K1.
Row 9: K1, *SKP, (yfwd, K2tog) twice, yfwd, K7, yfwd, (SKP, yfwd) twice, K2tog, rep from * to last st, inc1 K.
Row 11: sl1, *K1, psso, (yfwd, K2tog) twice, yfwd, K3, K2tog, K4, yfwd, (SKP, yfwd) twice, sl1, rep from * to last 2 sts, K1, psso, K1.
Rows 13 and 15: K1, *(yfwd, K2tog) twice, yfwd, K3, K2tog, SKP, K3, yfwd, (SKP, yfwd) twice, K1, rep from * to last st, K1.
Row 17: K1, *K1, (yfwd, SKP) twice, yfwd, K2, K2tog, SKP, K2, (yfwd, K2tog) twice, yfwd, K2, rep from * to last st, K1.
Row 19: K1, *K2, (yfwd, SKP) twice, yfwd, K1, K2tog, SKP, K1, yfwd, (K2tog, yfwd) twice, K3, rep from * to last st, K1.
Row 21: K1, *K3, (yfwd, SKP) twice, yfwd, K2tog, SKP, yfwd, (K2tog, yfwd) twice, K4, rep from * to last st, K1.
Row 23: K1, *K4, (yfwd, SKP) 3 times, yfwd, (K2tog, yfwd) twice, K3, K2tog, rep from * to last st, K1.
Row 24: P.
Rep these 24 rows.

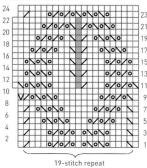

APPLE LEAVES lace

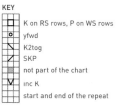

KEY

⊞	K on RS rows, P on WS rows
○	yfwd
◥	K2tog
◢	SKP
▦	not part of the chart
V	inc K
	start and end of the repeat

19-stitch repeat

CELL stitch (top section of picture)
DIAMOND EYELET pattern (middle section of picture)
APPLE LEAVES lace (bottom section of picture)

SLIP STITCH lace

Multiples of 4 sts plus 1
Row 1: (RS) K.
Row 2: *P4, yrn, rep from * to last st, P1.
Row 3: K1, *drop yrn on previous row, yfwd, sl1, K3, psso, rep from * to end.
Row 4: P.
Rep these 4 rows.

FAN lace

Multiples of 20 sts plus 1
make fan = K1 into first eyelet on row 5, pulling through a long loop, K1 into each of next 5 eyelets on rows 1, 3, and 5 in same way (see chart)
Row 1: (RS) K1, *K2, K2tog, yfwd, K1, yfwd, SKP, K5, K2tog, yfwd, K1, yfwd, SKP, K3, rep from * to end.
Rows 2, 4, and 6: P.
Row 3: K1, *K1, K2tog, yfwd, K3, yfwd, SKP, *K3, K2tog, yfwd, K3, yfwd, SKP, K2, rep from * to end.
Row 5: K1, *K2tog, yfwd, K5, yfwd, SKP, K1, rep from * to end.
Row 7: K1, *K5, make full fan, K10, K5, rep from * to end.
Row 8: *P5, P6 loops tog with next st, P9, P6 loops tog with next st, P4, rep from * to last st, P1.
Row 9: K.
Rows 10, 12, 14, and 16: P.
Row 11: K1, *yfwd, SKP, K5, K2tog, yfwd, K1, rep from * to end.
Row 13: K1, *K1, yfwd, SKP, K3, K2tog, yfwd, K3, yfwd, SKP, K3, K2tog, yfwd, K2, rep from * to end.
Row 15: K1, *K2, yfwd, SKP, K1, K2tog, yfwd, K5, yfwd, SKP, K1, K2tog, yfwd, K3, rep from * to end.
Row 17: K1, make half fan, *K10, make full fan, K10, make half fan, rep from * to end.
Row 18: *P3 loops tog with next st, P9, P6 loops tog (with next st), P9, rep from * to last st, P3 loops tog with last st.
Row 19: K.
Row 20: P.
Rep these 20 rows.

TWIN LEAF pattern

Multiples of 18 sts plus 1
Row 1: (RS) P1, *K4, K3tog, yfwd, K1, yfrn, P1, yfwd, K1, yfwd, sl2, K1, p2sso, K4, P1, rep from * to end.
Rows 2 and 4: *K1, P8, rep from * to last st, K1.
Row 3: P1, *K2, K3tog, (K1, yfwd) twice, K1, P1, K1, (yfwd, K1) twice, sl2, K1, p2sso, K2, P1, rep from * to end.
Row 5: P1, *K3tog, K2, yfwd, K1, yfwd, K2, P1, K2, yfwd, K1, yfwd, K2, sl2, K1, p2sso, P1, rep from * to end.
Row 6: As row 2.
Rep these 6 rows.

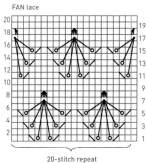

FAN lace

20-stitch repeat

KEY

	K on RS rows, P on WS rows
o	yfwd
/	K2tog
	P3tog
	P6tog
\	SKP
	start and end of the repeat

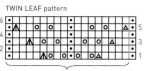

TWIN LEAF pattern

18-stitch repeat

KEY

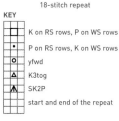

	K on RS rows, P on WS rows
•	P on RS rows, K on WS rows
o	yfwd
△	K3tog
⋏	SK2P
	start and end of the repeat

SLIP STITCH lace (top section of picture)
FAN lace (middle section of picture)
TWIN LEAF pattern (bottom section of picture)

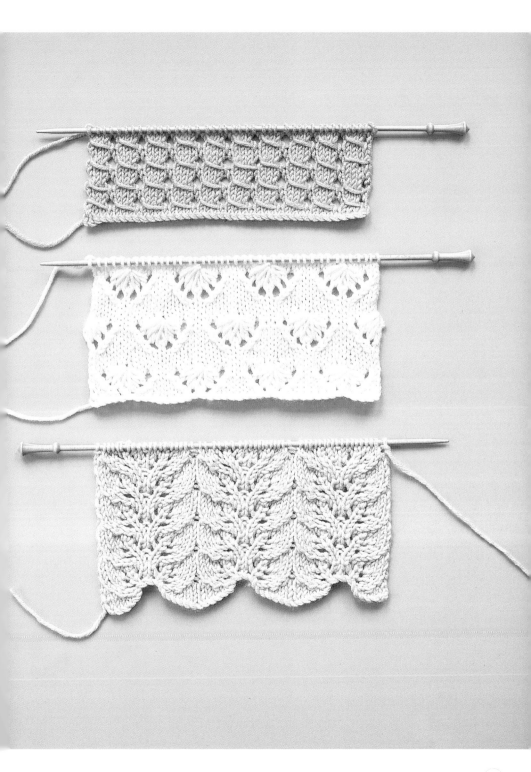

GOTHIC lace

Multiples of 10 sts plus 1

Row 1: (RS) K1, *yfwd, SKP, K5, K2tog, yfwd, K1, rep from * to end.

Row 2 and all WS rows: P.

Row 3: K2, *yfwd, SKP, K3, K2tog, yfwd, K3, rep from *, ending last rep K2.

Row 5: K3, *yfwd, SKP, K1, K2tog, yfwd, K5, rep from *, ending last rep K3.

Row 7: K4, *yfwd, SK2P, yfwd, K7, rep from *, ending last rep K4.

Row 9: K1, *yfwd, SKP, K2tog, yfwd, K1, rep from * to end.

Row 10: P.

Rows 11–18: Rep rows 9 and 10 four more times.

Row 19: As row 3.

Row 21: As row 5.

Row 23: As row 7.

Row 24: P.

Rep these 24 rows.

BRODERIE ANGLAIS lace

Multiples of 5 sts plus 2

Row 1: (WS) K.

Row 2: P.

Row 3: K1, *insert RHN into next st, yrn 3 times and pull loops through, dropping original st from LHN, rep from * to last st, K1.

Row 4: K1, *slip next 5 sts onto RHN, dropping extra loops, slip same sts back onto LHN, (K1, P1) twice, K1 into all 5 sts tog, rep from * to last st, K1.

Row 5: K.

Row 6: P.

Rep these 6 rows.

ST. JOHN'S WORT lace

Multiples of 6 sts

Row 1: (RS) *sl1, K2, psso, K3, rep from * to end.

Row 2: P4, *yrn, P5, rep from * to last st, yrn, P1.

Row 3: *K3, sl1, K2, psso, rep from * to end.

Row 4: P1, *yrn, P5, rep from * to last 4 sts, yrn, P4.

Rep these 4 rows.

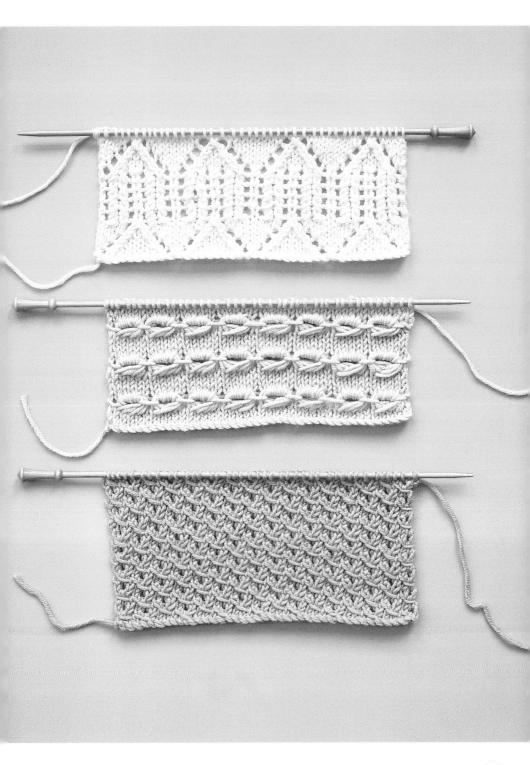

BEAD lace

Multiples of 6 sts plus 11

SP2P = slip 1 st, P2tog, pass slipped st over

SPP = slip 1 st, P1, pass slipped st over

Row 1: (RS) K3, K2tog, yfwd, K1, yfwd, SKP, *K1, K2tog, yfwd, K1, yfwd, SKP, rep from * to last 3 sts, K3.

Row 2: P2, (P1, slip st back onto LHN, lift 2nd st over it and slip it back onto RHN), *yfrn, P3, yrn, SP2P, rep from * to last 7 sts, yfrn, P3, yfrn, SPP, P2.

Row 3: K3, yfwd, SKP, K1, K2tog, yfwd, *K1, yfwd, SKP, K1, K2tog, yfwd, rep from * to last 3 sts, K3.

Row 4: P1, (P1, slip st back onto LHN, lift 2nd st over it and slip it back onto RHN), yfrn, *P1, yrn, SP2P, yfrn, P2, rep from * to last 7 sts, P1, yfrn, SP2P, yfrn, P1, yfrn, SPP, P1.
Rep these 4 rows.

SNOWDROP lace

Multiples of 8 sts plus 3

Rows 1 and 3: (RS) K1, K2tog, yfwd, *K5, yfwd, SK2P, yfwd, rep from * to last 8 sts, K5, yfwd, SKP, K1.

Row 2 and all WS rows: P.

Row 5: K3, *yfwd, SKP, K1, K2tog, yfwd, K3, rep from * to end.

Row 7: K1, K2tog, yfwd, *K1, yfwd, SK2P, yfwd, rep from * to last 4 sts, K1, yfwd, SKP, K1.

Row 8: P.
Rep these 8 rows.

ORIEL lace

Multiples of 12 sts plus 1

Row 1: (RS) P1, *SKP, K3, yfrn, P1, yon, K3, K2tog, P1, rep from * to end.

Row 2: K1, *P5, K1, rep from * to end.

Rows 3–6: Rep rows 1 and 2 twice more.

Row 7: P1, *yon, K3, K2tog, P1, SKP, K3, yfrn, P1, rep from * to end.

Row 8: As row 2.

Row 9: P2, *yon, K2, K2tog, P1, SKP, K2, yfrn, P3, rep from *, ending last rep P2.

Row 10: K2, *P4, K1, P4, K3, rep from *, ending last rep K2.

Row 11: P3, *yon, K1, K2tog, P1, SKP, K1, yfrn, P5, rep from *, ending last rep P3.

Row 12: K3, *P3, K1, P3, K5, rep from *, ending last rep K3.

Row 13: P4, *yon, K2tog, P1, SKP, yfrn, P7, rep from *, ending last rep P4.

Row 14: K4, *P2, K1, P2, K7, rep from *, ending last rep K4.

Row 15: As row 7.

Row 16: As row 2.

Rows 17–20: Rep rows 15 and 16 twice more.

Row 21: As row 1.

Row 22: As row 2.

Row 23: P1, *SKP, K2, yfrn, P3, yon, K2, K2tog, P1, rep from * to end.

Row 24: K1, *P4, K3, P4, K1, rep from * to end.

Row 25: P1, *SKP, K1, yfrn, P5, yon, K1, K2tog, P1, rep from * to end.

Row 26: K1, *P3, K5, P3, K1, rep from * to end.

Row 27: P1, * SKP, yfrn, P7, yon, K2tog, P1, rep from * to end.

Row 28: K1, *P2, K7, P2, K1, rep from * to end.
Rep these 28 rows.

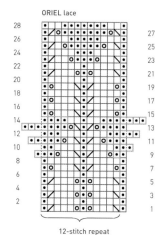

ORIEL lace

12-stitch repeat

KEY

	K on RS rows, P on WS rows
•	P on RS rows, K on WS rows
O	yfrn or yon
/	K2tog
\	SKP
	start and end of the repeat

BEAD lace (top section of picture)

SNOWDROP lace (middle section of picture)

ORIEL lace (bottom section of picture)

HORSESHOE lace

Multiples of 10 sts plus 1

Row 1: (RS) K1, *yrn, K3, SK2P, K3, yfwd, K1, rep from * to end.

Rows 2 and all WS rows: P.

Row 3: K1, *K1, yfwd, K2, SK2P, K2, yfwd, K2, rep from * to end.

Row 5: K1, *K2, yfwd, K1, SK2P, K1, yfwd, K3, rep from * to end.

Row 7: K1, *K3, yfwd, SK2P, yfwd, K4, rep from * to end.

Row 8: P.

Rep these 8 rows.

CROWN OF GLORY lace

Multiples of 14 sts plus 1

Row 1: (RS) K1, *SKP, K9, K2tog, K1, rep from * to end.

Row 2: *P1, P2tog, P7, P2tog tbl, rep from * to last st, P1.

Row 3: K1, *SKP, K2, yrn 3 times, K3, K2tog, K1, rep from * to end.

Row 4: *P1, P2tog, P2, (K1, P1, K1, P1, K1) into the yrn 3 times, P1, P2tog tbl, rep from * to last st, P1.

Row 5: K1, *SKP, K6, K2tog, K1, rep from * to end.

Row 6: *P1, P2tog, P6, rep from *, ending last rep P1.

Row 7: K1, *K1, (yfwd, K1) 6 times, K1, rep from * to end.

Rows 8 and 11: P.

Rows 9 and 10: K.

Row 12: K.

Rep these 12 rows.

FEATHER AND FAN lace

Multiples of 13 sts plus 15

Row 1: (WS) Using contrast color, K.

Row 2: Using main color, K7, *(K1, P1) 3 times into next st, K12, rep from * to last 8 sts, (K1, P1) 3 times into next st, K7.

Row 3: K7, *P6, K12, rep from * to last 13 sts, P6, K7.

Row 4: K.

Row 5: As row 3.

Row 6: K1, K2tog twice, K4, *yfwd, K2, yfwd, K4, K2tog 4 times, K4, rep from *, ending last rep K2tog twice, K1.

Row 7: K5, *P8, K8, rep from * to last 13 sts, P8, K5.

Row 8: K1, K2tog twice, *(K2tog tbl, yfwd, K1, yfwd) twice, K2tog 5 times, rep from *, ending last rep K2tog 3 times, K1.

Row 9: K3, *P9, K4, rep from * to last 12 sts, P9, K3.

Row 10: K1, K2tog, K2tog tbl, *(yfwd, K1) 5 times, yfwd, K2tog 3 times, K2tog tbl, rep from *, ending last rep K2tog twice, K1.

Row 11: K1, *P2tog tbl, P11, P2tog, rep from * to last st, K1.

Rows 12 and 13: Using contrast color, K.

Rep rows 2–13.

DIAMOND lace

Multiples of 6 sts plus 1

Row 1: (RS) K1, *K2tog, yfwd, K1, yfwd, SKP, K1, rep from * to end .

Rows 2 and all WS rows: P.

Row 3: K2tog, yfwd, *K3, yfwd, sl2k, K1, p2sso, yfwd, rep from * to last 5 sts, K3, yfwd, SKP.

Row 5: K1, *yfwd, SKP, K1, K2tog, yfwd, K1, rep from * to end.

Row 7: K2, *yfwd, sl2k, K1, p2sso, yfwd, K3, rep from *, ending last rep K2.

Row 8: P.

Rep these 8 rows.

VINE lace

Multiples of 9 sts plus 4

Row 1: (WS) P.

Row 2: K3, *yfwd, K2, SKP, K2tog, K2, yfwd, K1, rep from * to last st, K1.

Row 3: P.

Row 4: K2, *yfwd, K2, SKP, K2tog, K2, yfwd, K1, rep from * to last 2 sts, K2.

Rep these 4 rows.

OGEE lace

Multiples of 24 sts plus 1

Row 1: (RS) *K2, yfwd, K2tog, K1, K2tog, K3, yfwd, SKP, yfrn, P1, yon, K2, yfwd, (SKP, K1) twice, SKP, yfwd, K1, rep from * to last st, K1.

Row 2: P1, *P7, yrn, P2tog, P5, yrn, P2tog, P8, rep from * to end.

Row 3: *K1, yfwd, K2tog, K1, K2tog, K3, yfwd, SKP, (K1, yfwd) twice, K3, yfwd, (SKP, K1) twice, SKP, yfwd, rep from * to last st, K1.

Row 4: P1, *P6, yrn, P2tog, P7, yrn, P2tog, P7, rep from * to end.

Row 5: *K3, K2tog, K3, yfwd, SKP, K1, yfwd, (K3, yfwd) twice, SKP, K1, SKP, K2, rep from * to last st, K1.

Row 6: P1, *P5, yrn, P2tog, P9, yrn, P2tog, P6, rep from * to end.

Row 7: *K2, K2tog, K3, yfwd, SKP, K3, yfwd, K1, yfwd, K5, yfwd, (SKP, K1) twice, rep from * to last st, K1.

Row 8: P1, *P4, yrn, P2tog, P11, yrn, P2tog, P5, rep from * to end.

Row 9: *K1, K2tog, K3, yfwd, SKP, (K3, yfwd) twice, K5, yfwd, SKP, K1, SKP, rep from * to last st, K1.

Row 10: P1, *P3, yrn, P2tog, P13, yrn, P2tog, P4, rep from * to end.

Row 11: SKP, *K3, yfwd, SKP, K1, SKP, yfwd, K2, yfwd, K1, yfwd, K2, yfwd, K2tog, K3, yfwd, SKP, K1, SK2P, rep from *, ending last rep SKP.

Row 12: P1, *P2, yrn, P2tog, P15, yrn, P2tog, P3, rep from * to end.

Row 13: SKP, *K2, yfwd, SKP, K5, yfwd, K3, yfwd, K7, yfwd, SKP, SK2P, rep from *, ending last rep SKP twice.

Row 14: K1, *P1, yrn, P2tog, P17, yrn, P2tog, P1, K1, rep from * to end.

Row 15: *P1, yon, K2, yfwd, (SKP, K1) twice, SKP, yfwd, K3, yfwd, K2tog, K1, K2tog, K3, yfwd, SKP, yrn, rep from * to last st, P1.

Row 16: As row 12.

Row 17: *K1, yfwd, K3, yfwd, (SKP, K1) twice, SKP, yfwd, K1, yfwd, K2tog, K1, K2tog, K3, yfwd, SKP, K1, yfwd, rep from * to last st, K1.

Row 18: As row 10.

Row 19: *K2, yfwd, K3, yfwd, SKP, K1, SKP, K5, K2tog, K3, yfwd, SKP, K1, yfwd, K1, rep from * to last st, K1.

Row 20: As row 8.

Row 21: *K1, yfwd, K5, yfwd, SKP, K1, SKP, K3, K2tog, K3, yfwd, SKP, K3, yfwd, rep from * to last st, K1.

Row 22: As row 6.

Row 23: *K2, yfwd, K5, yfwd, (SKP, K1) twice, K2tog, K3, yfwd, SKP, K3, yfwd, K1, rep from * to last st, K1.

Row 24: As row 4.

Row 25: *K1, yfwd, K2, yfwd, K2tog, K3, yfwd, SKP, K1, SK2P, K3, yfwd, SKP, K1, SKP, yfwd, K2, yfwd, rep from * to last st, K1.

Row 26: As row 2.

Row 27: *K2, yfwd, K7, yfwd, SKP, SK2P, K2, yfwd, SKP, K5, yfwd, K1, rep from * to last st, K1.

Row 28: P1, *P8, yrn, P2tog, P1, K1, P1, yrn, P2tog, P9, rep from * to end.

Rep these 28 rows.

OGEE lace

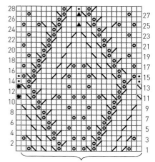

24-stitch repeat

KEY

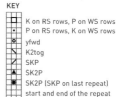

K on RS rows, P on WS rows
P on RS rows, K on WS rows
yfwd
K2tog
SKP
SK2P
SK2P (SKP on last repeat)
start and end of the repeat

DIAMOND lace (top section of picture)
VINE lace (middle section of picture)
OGEE lace (bottom section of picture)

PRINT O' THE WAVE lace

Multiples of 22 sts plus 3
Row 1: (RS) K4, *K2tog, K3, (yfwd, K2tog) twice, yfwd, K13, rep from *, ending last rep K12.
Rows 2 and all WS rows: P.
Row 3: K3, *K2tog, K3, yfwd, K1, yfwd, (SKP, yfwd) twice, K3, SKP, K7, rep from * to end.
Row 5: K2, *K2tog, (K3, yfwd) twice, (SKP, yfwd) twice, K3, SKP, K5, rep from * to last st, K1.
Row 7: K1, *K2tog, K3, yfwd, K5, yfwd, (SKP, yfwd) twice, K3, SKP, K3, rep from * to last 2 sts, K2.
Row 9: *K12, yfwd, (SKP, yfwd) twice, K3, SKP, K1, rep from * to last 3 sts, K3.
Row 11: *K7, K2tog, K3, (yfwd, K2tog) twice, yfwd, K1, yfwd, K3, SKP, rep from * to last 3 sts, K3.
Row 13: K6, *K2tog, K3, (yfwd, K2tog) twice, (yfwd, K3) twice, SKP, K5, rep from *, ending last rep K2.
Row 15: K5, *K2tog, K3, (yfwd, K2tog) twice, yfwd, K5, yfwd, K3, SKP, K3, rep from *, ending last rep K1.
Row 16: P.
Rep these 16 rows.

EYELET stitch

Multiples of 4 sts plus 4
Row 1: (RS) K4, *yrn twice, K4, rep from * to end.
Row 2: P2, *P2tog, P1, K1, P2tog, rep from * to last 2 sts, P2.
Row 3: K2, yfwd, *K4, yrn twice, rep from * to last 6 sts, K4, yfwd, K2.
Row 4: P3, *P2tog twice, P1, K1, rep from * to last 7 sts, P2tog twice, P3.
Rep these 4 rows.

TRAVELING VINE lace

Multiples of 10 sts plus 1
Row 1: (RS) K1, *K2tog, K4, yfwd, K1, yfwd, SKP, K1, rep from * to end.
Row 2 and all WS rows: P.
Row 3: K1, *K2tog, K3, (yfwd, K1) twice, SKP, K1, rep from * to end.
Row 5: K1, *K2tog, K2, yfwd, K1, yfwd, K2, SKP, K1, rep from * to end.
Row 7: K1, *K2tog, (K1, yfwd) twice, K3, SKP, K1, rep from * to end.
Row 9: K1, *K2tog, yfwd, K1, yfwd, K4, SKP, K1, rep from * to end.
Row 11: K1, *K2tog, (K1, yfwd) twice, K3, SKP, K1, rep from * to end.
Row 13: K1, *K2tog, K2, yfwd, K1, yfwd, K2, SKP, K1, rep from * to end.
Row 15: K1, *K2tog, K3, (yfwd, K1) twice, SKP, K1, rep from * to end.
Row 16: P.
Rep these 16 rows.

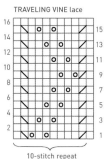

TRAVELING VINE lace

10-stitch repeat

KEY

	K on RS rows, P on WS rows
o	yfwd
/	K2tog
\	SKP
	start and end of the repeat

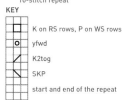

PRINT O' THE WAVE lace (top section of picture)
EYELET stitch (middle section of picture)
TRAVELING VINE lace (bottom section of picture)

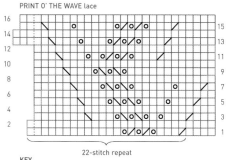

PRINT O' THE WAVE lace

22-stitch repeat

KEY

	K on RS rows, P on WS rows
o	yfwd
/	K2tog
\	SKP
	start and end of the repeat

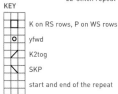

CHEVRON lace

Multiples of 12 sts plus 1
Row 1 and all WS rows: P.
Row 2: K4, *K2tog, yfwd, K1, yfwd, SKP, K7, rep from *, ending last rep K4.
Row 4: K3, *K2tog, yfwd, K3, yfwd, SKP, K5, rep from *, ending last rep K3.
Row 6: K2, *(K2tog, yfwd) twice, K1, (yfwd, SKP) twice, K3, rep from *, ending last rep K2.
Row 8: K1, *(K2tog, yfwd) twice, K3, (yfwd, SKP) twice, K1, rep from * to end.
Row 10: K2tog, *yfwd, K2tog, yfwd, K5, yfwd, SKP, yfwd, SK2P, rep from *, ending last rep SKP.
Row 12: K1, *K2tog, yfwd, K1, yfwd, SKP, K1, rep from * to end.
Row 14: K2tog, *yfwd, K3, yfwd, SK2P, rep from *, ending last rep SKP.
Rep these 14 rows.

LACE mesh

Multiples of 3 sts (minimum of 6 sts)
Row 1: (RS) K2, *yfwd, sl1, K2, psso the K2, rep from * to last st, K1.
Row 2: P.
Row 3: K1, *sl1, K2, psso the K2, yfwd, rep from * to last 2 sts, K2.
Row 4: P.
Rep these 4 rows.

FIR CONE lace

Multiples of 12 sts plus 1
Row 1: (RS) P1, *P3, K5, P4, rep from * to end.
Row 2 and all WS rows: P.
Row 3: P2tog, *P2, K2, yfwd, K1, yfwd, K2, P2, P3tog, rep from *, ending last rep P2tog.
Row 5: P2tog, *P1, K2, yfwd, K3, yfwd, K2, P1, P3tog, rep from *, ending last rep P2tog.
Row 7: P2tog, *K2, yfwd, K5, yfwd, K2, P2tog, rep from *, ending last rep P2tog.
Row 8: P.
Rep these 8 rows.

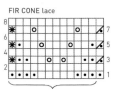

FIR CONE lace

12-stitch repeat

KEY

	K on RS rows, P on WS rows
•	P on RS rows, K on WS rows
o	yfwd
⁄	P2tog
✳	P3tog (P2tog on last repeat)
	start and end of the repeat

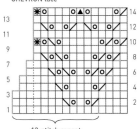

CHEVRON lace

12-stitch repeat

KEY

	K on RS rows, P on WS rows
o	yfwd
╲	K2tog
╱	SKP
▲	SK2P
✳	SK2P (SKP on last repeat)
	start and end of the repeat

CHEVRON lace (top section of picture)
LACE mesh (middle section of picture)
FIR CONE lace (bottom section of picture)

208 knitted lace

Textured colorwork

Simple stripes in well-thought-out color combinations are a very effective way of creating a colorful piece of knitting. The patterns in this section go a stage further and introduce the element of texture too. The effects are much easier to achieve than they appear. With a simple slip stitch (always worked purlwise) and only one color worked on each row, all sorts of clever textures quickly start to appear.

Plain, single-colored yarns will produce the best effects with these stitches. Also, choose colors that are not too close in tonal range; otherwise they will tend to merge and not bring out the pattern. To work stitches that involve more intricacy than slip stitch, such as Star stitch and Garland stitch, you will probably prefer a yarn with elasticity.

Note: Throughout the Textured colorwork section, A = color A; B = color B; C = color C.

TWO-COLOR LOOP stitch
Multiples of 2 sts plus 1
Row 1: (RS) Using A, K.
Row 2: Using A, P.
Row 3: Using B, K1, *sl1, K1, rep from * to end.
Row 4: As row 3.
Row 5: Using B, K.
Row 6: Using B, P.
Row 7: Using A, K2, sl1, *K1, sl1, rep from * to last 2 sts, K2.
Row 8: Using A, P1, K1, *sl1, K1, rep from * to last st, P1.
Rep these 8 rows.

MOSS TWEED stitch
Multiples of 2 sts
Double-pointed needles are useful
Row 1: (RS) Using A, *K1, sl1, rep from * to end; return to beg of row.
Row 2: Using B, *sl1, K1, rep from * to end.
Row 3: Using A, *sl1, ybk, K1, yfwd, rep from * to end; return to beg of row.
Row 4: Using B, *K1, yfwd, sl1, ybk, rep from * to end.
Row 5: Using A, *sl1, K1, rep from * to end; return to beg of row.
Row 6: Using B, *K1, sl1, rep from * to end.
Row 7: Using A, *K1, yfwd, sl1, ybk, rep from * to end; return to beg of row.
Row 8: Using B, *sl1, ybk, K1, yfwd, rep from * to end.
Rep these 8 rows.

LADDER stitch
Multiples of 6 sts plus 5
Row 1: (RS) Using A, K2, *sl1, K5, rep from * to last 3 sts, sl1, K2.
Row 2: Using A, P2, *sl1, P5, rep from * to last 3 sts, sl1, P2.
Row 3: Using B, *K5, sl1, rep from * to last 5 sts, K5.
Row 4: Using B, *K5, yfwd, sl1, ybk, rep from * to last 5 sts, K5.
Rep these 4 rows.

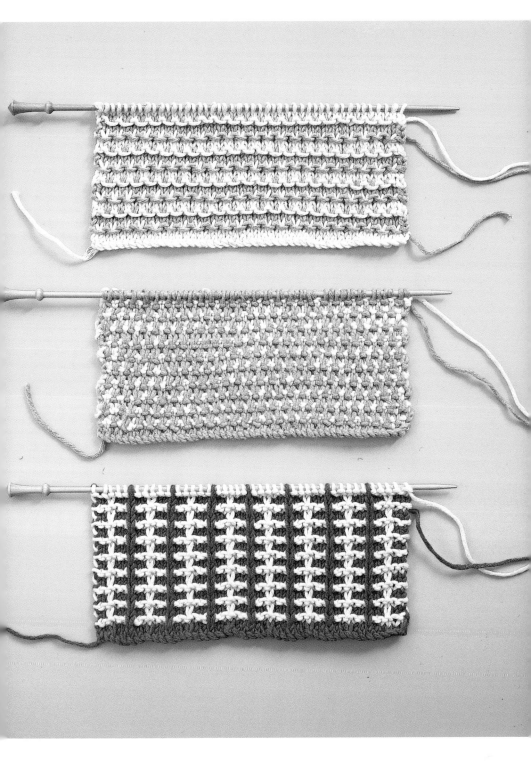

CHEVRON stripes

Multiples of 14 sts

Row 1: (RS) K.

Row 2: P.

Row 3: *K1, K1 but leave on LHN, K into st below and transfer both sts to RHN, K4, SK2P, K4, K into st below next st, K1 into st on LHN and transfer both sts to RHN, rep from * to end.

Row 4: P.

Rep these 4 rows.

TAPESTRY stitch

Multiples of 4 sts plus 3

Row 1: (WS) Using A, P.

Row 2: Using B, K1, yfwd, sl1, ybk, K1, *sl1, K1, yfwd, sl1, ybk, K1, rep from * to end.

Row 3: Using B, P3, *sl1, P3, rep from * to end.

Row 4: Using A, K1, *sl1, K3, rep from * to last 2 sts, sl1, K1.

Row 5: As row 1.

Row 6: Using B, K1, sl1, K1, *yfwd, sl1, ybk, K1, sl1, K1, rep from * to end.

Row 7: Using B, P1, *sl1, P3, rep from * to last 2 sts, sl1, P1.

Row 8: Using A, K3, *sl1, K3, rep from * to end.

Rep these 8 rows.

TWO-COLOR RICE stitch

Multiples of 2 sts

Double-pointed needles are useful

Row 1: (RS) Using A, *K1, sl1, rep from * to end; return to beg of row.

Row 2: Using B, *P1, K1, rep from * to end.

Row 3: Using A, *P1, sl1k, rep from * to end; return to beg of row.

Row 4: Using B, *K1, P1, rep from * to end.

Rep these 4 rows.

CHEVRON stripes (top section of picture)
TAPESTRY stitch (middle section of picture)
TWO-COLOR RICE stitch (bottom section of picture)

FUCHSIA pattern

Multiples of 4 sts

Rows 1 and 3: (RS) Using A, K.

Rows 2 and 4: Using A, P.

Row 5: Using B, *K3, insert RHN into next st in row 1 and pull through a loop, K1, bring loop over last st, rep from * to end.

Rows 6 and 8: Using B, P.

Row 7: Using B, K.

Row 9: Using A, *K1, insert RHN into next st in row 5 and pull through a loop, K1, bring loop over last st, K2, rep from * to end.

Rep rows 2–9.

BRICK stitch

Multiples of 4 sts plus 3

Row 1: (RS) Using A, K.

Row 2: Using A, P.

Row 3: Using B, K3, *sl1, K3, rep from * to end.

Row 4: Using B, K3, *yfwd, sl1, ybk, K3, rep from * to end.

Row 5: Using A, K2, *sl1, K1, rep from * to last st, K1.

Row 6: Using A, P2, *sl1, P1, rep from * to last st, P1.

Row 7: Using B, K1, *sl1, K3, rep from * to last 2 sts, sl1, K1.

Row 8: Using B, K1, *yfwd, sl1, ybk, K3, rep from * to last 2 sts, yfwd, sl1, ybk, K1.

Row 9: As row 1.

Row 10: As row 2.

Row 11: As row 7.

Row 12: As row 8.

Row 13: As row 5.

Row 14: As row 6.

Row 15: As row 3.

Row 16: As row 4.

Rep these 16 rows.

THREE-COLOR LINEN stitch

Multiples of 2 sts

Row 1: (RS) Using A, *yfwd, sl1, ybk, K1, rep from * to end.

Row 2: Using B, *ybk, sl1, yfwd, P1, rep from * to end.

Row 3: Using C, as row 1.

Row 4: Using A, as row 2.

Row 5: Using B, as row 1.

Row 6: Using C, as row 2.

Rep these 6 rows.

TIP Although this stitch is not reversible, the reverse is very attractive.

FUCHSIA pattern (top section of picture)
BRICK stitch (middle section of picture)
THREE-COLOR LINEN stitch (bottom section of picture)

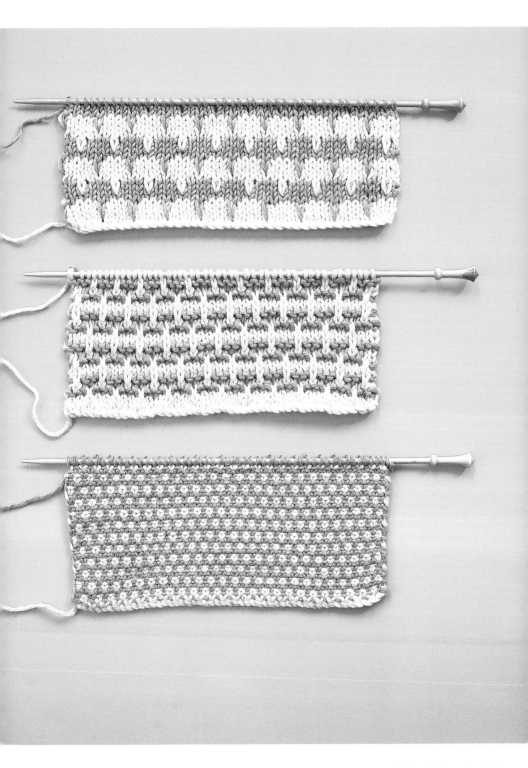

SLIP STITCH rows

Multiples of 6 sts plus 5

Row 1: (RS) Using A, K.
Row 2: Using A, P.
Row 3: Using B, K2, *sl1, K1, rep from * to last st, K1.
Row 4: Using B, K1, *K1, yfwd, sl1, ybk, K1, yfwd, sl1, P1, sl1, ybk, rep from * to last 4 sts, K1, yfwd, sl1, ybk, K2.
Rows 5 and 7: Using A, K5, *sl1, K5, rep from * to end.
Rows 6 and 8: Using A, P5, *sl1, P5, rep from * to end.
Row 9: Using A, as row 1.
Row 10: Using A, as row 2.
Row 11: Using B, K1, *sl1, K1, rep from * to end.
Row 12: Using B, K1, *yfwd, sl1, P1, sl1, ybk, K1, yfwd, sl1, ybk, K1, rep from * to last 4 sts, yfwd, sl1, P1, sl1, ybk, K1.
Rows 13 and 15: Using A, K2, *sl1, K5, rep from * to last 3 sts, sl1, K2.
Rows 14 and 16: Using A, P2, *sl1, P5, rep from * to last 3 sts, sl1, P2.
Rep these 16 rows.

GARLAND stitch

Multiples of 7 sts plus 2

Rows 1 and 5: (RS) Using A, K.
Rows 2 and 6: Using A, P.
Rows 3, 4, 7, and 8: Using B, K.
Row 9: Using A, *K3, insert RHN into row 3 below 2nd st and pull through a loop onto RHN, K1, sl1, K2, pull another loop through same st on row 3, rep from * to last 2 sts, K2.
Row 10: Using A, P2, *P2tog, P1, sl1, P1, P2tog, P2, rep from * to end.
Rep these 10 rows.

TWO-COLOR STAR stitch

Multiples of 4 sts plus 3

make star = K into front of next 3tog, K into back of same 3tog, K into front of same 3tog

Row 1: (RS) Using A, P.
Row 2: Using A, * make star, K1, rep from * to last 3 sts, make star.
Row 3: Using B, P.
Row 4: Using B, K2, *make star, K1, rep from * to last st, K1.
Rep these 4 rows.

TIP To work this stitch, choose an elastic yarn or keep the tension fairly loose.

SLIP STITCH rows (top section of picture)
GARLAND stitch (middle section of picture)
TWO-COLOR STAR stitch (bottom section of picture)

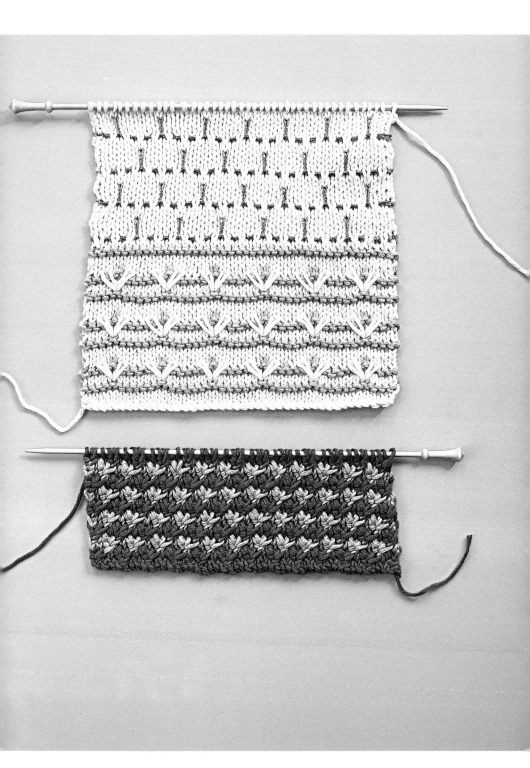

RIDGED stripes

Multiples of 4 sts plus 3

Row 1: (RS) Using A, K.
Row 2: Using A, P.
Row 3: Using B, K3, *sl1, K3, rep from * to end.
Row 4: Using B, P3, *sl1, P3, rep from * to end.
Row 5: Using C, K1, *sl1, K3, rep from * to last 2 sts, sl1, K1.
Row 6: Using C, P1, *sl1, P3, rep from * to last 2 sts, sl1, P1.
Row 7: Using B, as row 3.
Row 8: Using B, as row 4.
Row 9: Using A, as row 5.
Row 10: Using A, as row 6.
Rep these 10 rows.

BIRD'S EYE stitch

Multiples of 2 sts

Row 1: (RS) Using A, *sl1, K1, rep from * to end.
Row 2: Using A, P.
Row 3: Using B, *K1, sl1, rep from * to end.
Row 4: Using B, P.
Rep these 4 rows.

CROSSED COLOR stitch

Multiples of 2 sts plus 1

Rows 1 and 5: (RS) Using A, K.
Rows 2 and 6: Using A, K.
Row 3: Using B, *K1, sl1, rep from * to last st, K1.
Row 4: Using B, *K1, yfwd, sl1, ybk, rep from * to last st, K1.
Row 7: Using B, *sl1, K1, rep from * to last st, sl1.
Row 8: Using B, *sl1, ybk, K1, yfwd, rep from * to last st, sl1.
Rep these 8 rows.

RIDGED stripes (top section of picture)
BIRD'S EYE stitch (middle section of picture)
CROSSED COLOR stitch (bottom section of picture)

RIDGED CHECK stitch

Multiples of 4 sts plus 3

Row 1: (WS) Using A, P.

Row 2: Using B, K3, *sl1k, K3, rep from * to end.

Row 3: Using B, P3, *sl1, P3, rep from * to end.

Row 4: Using B, as row 2.

Row 5: Using B, P.

Row 6: Using A, as row 2.

Row 7: Using A, as row 3.

Row 8: Using A, K3, *sl1k, K3, rep from * to end.

Rep these 8 rows.

TWO-COLOR TWEED stitch

Multiples of 3 sts

Row 1: (RS) Using A, *sl1, K2, rep from * to end.

Row 2: Using A, K.

Row 3: Using B, *K2, sl1, rep from * to end.

Row 4: Using B, K.

Rep these 4 rows.

THREE-COLOR TWEED stitch

Multiples of 3 sts plus 1

Row 1: (WS) Using A, K.

Row 2: Using B, K3, *sl1k, K2, rep from * to last st, K1.

Row 3: Using B, K3, *yfwd, sl1, ybk, K2, rep from * to last st, K1.

Row 4: Using C, *K2, sl1k, rep from * to last st, K1.

Row 5: Using C, K1, *yfwd, sl1, ybk, K2, rep from * to end.

Row 6: Using A, K1, *sl1k, K2, rep from * to end.

Row 7: Using A, *K2, yfwd, sl1, ybk, rep from * to last st, K1.

Rep rows 2–7.

RIDGED CHECK stitch (top section of picture)
TWO-COLOR TWEED stitch (middle section of picture)
THREE-COLOR TWEED stitch (bottom section of picture)

SLIP STITCH stripes

Multiples of 4 sts plus 3
Row 1: (WS) Using A, P.
Row 2: Using B, K2, *sl1k, K1, rep from * to last st, K1.
Row 3: Using B, P2, *sl1, P1, rep from * to last st, P1.
Row 4: Using C, K1, *sl1k, K1, rep from * to end.
Row 5: Using C, P.
Row 6: Using D, K1, *sl1k, K3, rep from * to last 2 sts, sl1k, K1.
Row 7: Using D, P1, *sl1, P3, rep from * to last 2 sts, sl1, P1.
Row 8: Using B, K2, *sl3k, K1, rep from * to last st, K1.
Row 9: Using B, *P3, sl1, rep from * to last 3 sts, P3.
Row 10: Using A, K1, *sl1k, K3, rep from * to last 2 sts, sl1k, K1.
Rep these 10 rows.

TWO-COLOR HURDLE stitch

Multiples of 4 sts plus 3
Row 1: (WS) Using A, K.
Row 2: Using B, K3, *sl1k, K3, rep from * to end.
Row 3: Using B, K3, *yfwd, sl1k, ybk, K3, rep from * to end.
Row 4: Using A, K1, *sl1k, K3, rep from * to last 2 sts, sl1k, K1.
Row 5: Using A, K1, *yfwd, sl1k, ybk, K3, rep from * to last 2 sts, yfwd, sl1k, ybk, K1.
Rep rows 2–5.

TWO-COLOR GRANITE stitch

Multiples of 2 sts plus 1
Row 1: (RS) Using A, K.
Row 2: Using B, *K1, sl1, rep from * to last st, K1.
Row 3: Using B, *K1, yfwd, sl1, ybk, rep from * to last st, K1.
Rows 4 and 5: Using A, K.
Row 6: Using B, K1, *K1, sl1, rep from * to last 2 sts, K2.
Row 7: Using B, K2, *yfwd, sl1, ybk, K1, rep from * to last st, K1.
Row 8: Using A, K.
Rep these 8 rows.

SLIP STITCH stripes (top section of picture)
TWO-COLOR HURDLE stitch (middle section of picture)
TWO-COLOR GRANITE stitch (bottom section of picture)

NET pattern
Multiples of 8 sts plus 4
Row 1: (RS) Using A, K3; *using B, K2; using A, K6; rep from * to last st; using B, K1.
Row 2: Using B, K1 and leave yarn at back of work; *using A, P6; using B, K2 and leave yarn at back of work; rep from * to last 3 sts; using A, P3.
Row 3: Using B, K1; *using A, K6; (using B, K1 with RHN under B from previous row) twice; rep from * to last 3 sts; using A, K3.
Row 4: Using A, P3; *using B, K2 and leave yarn at back of work; using A, P6; rep from * to last st; using B, K1.
Row 5: Using A, K3; *(using B, K1 with RHN under B from previous row) twice; using A, K6; rep from * to last st; using B, K1.
Rep rows 2–5.

LATTICE pattern
Multiples of 6 sts plus 2
Row 1: (WS) Using A, K.
Row 2: Using B, K1, sl1, *K4, sl2, rep from * to last 6 sts, K4, sl1, K1.
Row 3: Using B, P1, sl1, *P4, sl2, rep from * to last 6 sts, P4, sl1, P1.
Row 4: Using A, as row 2.
Row 5: Using A, K1, yfwd, sl1, ybk, *K4, yfwd, sl2, ybk, rep from * to last 6 sts, K4, yfwd, sl1, ybk, K1.
Row 6: Using B, K3, *sl2, K4, rep from * to last 5 sts, sl2, K3.
Row 7: Using B, P3, *sl2, P4, rep from * to last 5 sts, sl2, P3.
Row 8: Using A, as row 6.
Row 9: Using A, K3, *yfwd, sl2, ybk, K4, rep from * to last 5 sts, yfwd, sl2, ybk, K3.
Rep rows 2–9.

CHAIN pattern
Multiples of 8 sts plus 6
Row 1: (RS) Using A, K.
Row 2: Using A, P.
Rows 3 and 4: Using B, K.
Row 5: Using A, K6, *sl2, K6, rep from * to end.
Row 6: Using A, P6, *sl2, P6, rep from * to end.
Row 7: Using B, as row 5.
Row 8: Using B, K.
Row 9: Using A, K.
Row 10: Using A, P.
Rows 11 and 12: Using C, K.
Row 13: Using A, K2, *sl2, K6, rep from * to last 4 sts, sl2, K2.
Row 14: Using A, P2, *sl2, P6, rep from * to last 4 sts, sl2, P2.
Row 15: Using C, as row 13.
Row 16: Using C, K.
Rep these 16 rows.

NET pattern (top section of picture)
LATTICE pattern (middle section of picture)
CHAIN pattern (bottom section of picture)

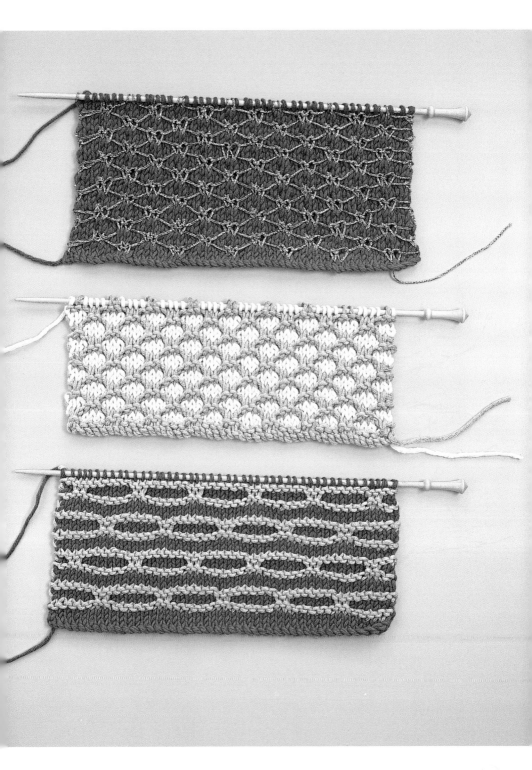

RIBBON stitch

Multiples of 4 sts plus 3

Row 1: (WS) Using A, P.

Row 2: Using B, K1, *sl1, K3, rep from * to last 2 sts, sl1, K1.

Row 3: Using B, K1, *yfwd, sl1, ybk, K1, K1 wrapping yrn 3 times, K1, rep from * to last 2 sts, yfwd, sl1, ybk, K1.

Row 4: Using A, K3, *sl1 dropping extra loops, K3, rep from * to end.

Rows 5 and 7: Using A, P3, *ybk, sl1, yfwd, P3, rep from * to end.

Rows 6 and 8: Using A, K3, *sl1, K3, rep from * to end.

Rep these 8 rows.

TWO-COLOR OAK stitch

Multiples of 2 sts

Row 1: (RS) Using A, K.

Row 2: Using A, K.

Row 3: Using B, *K1 through next st on previous row, K1, rep from * to end.

Row 4: Using B, K.

Row 5: Using A, *K1, K1 through next st on previous row, rep from * to end.

Row 6: Using A, K.

Rep rows 3–6.

THREE-COLOR OAK stitch

Multiples of 4 sts

Row 1: (WS) Using A, P.

Row 2: Using B, *K3, sl1, rep from * to end.

Row 3: Using B, *yfwd, sl1, ybk, K3, rep from * to end.

Row 4: Using C, *K1, sl1, K2, rep from * to end.

Row 5: Using C, *K2, yfwd, sl1, ybk, K1, rep from * to end.

Row 6: Using A, as row 2.

Row 7: Using A, as row 3.

Row 8: Using B, as row 4.

Row 9: Using B, as row 5.

Row 10: Using C, as row 2.

Row 11: Using C, as row 3.

Row 12: Using A, as row 4.

Row 13: Using A, as row 5.

Rep rows 2–13.

RIBBON stitch (top section of picture)
TWO-COLOR OAK stitch (middle section of picture)
THREE-COLOR OAK stitch (bottom section of picture)

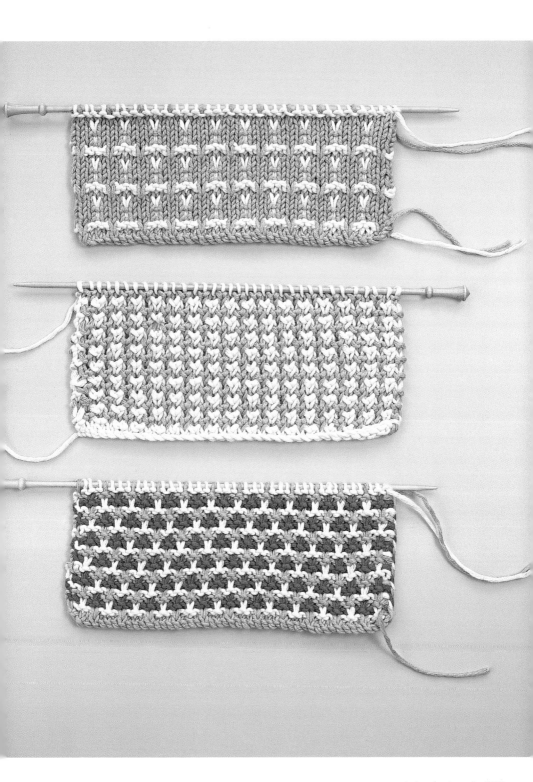

Fair Isle

The now generic term Fair Isle applies to multicolored Stockinette stitch, worked in just two colors on one row, loosely stranding the color not in use in short loops, or floats, across the back of the work. This creates a warm, double thickness.

Traditionally the patterns were worked in soft shades of lace-weight Shetland wool with subtle color changes every few rows. If you want the same effect, choose as few as six colors—two of a similar tone, a darker or lighter shade of each, a total contrast, and a background color. For a different but equally appealing result, choose brighter super fine-weight cottons or silks. A random-dyed yarn on a single plain background can also give a stunning effect.

It might look complicated, but once you've set up a pattern it's easy to remember or work from previous rows because of the symmetries and the way the patterns often progress along diagonal lines. The patterns are often combined in horizontal bands, but they can also be worked as single bands on an otherwise plain piece or as vertical panels. The larger patterns, such as Norwegian stars, make dramatic single motifs, and the overall checkerboard designs are equally impressive.

Although these samples have been worked flat, you could try knitting Fair Isle in the round. This is much quicker, as you don't need to turn the knitting, sew in as many yarn ends, or sew up seams; and the right side is always facing you.

Note: Throughout the Fair Isle section, A = color A; B = color B.

NORWEGIAN STAR pattern

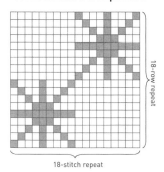

18-row repeat

18-stitch repeat

STRIPED ribbing
Multiples of 2 sts plus 1
All rows: (RS) *Using A, K1; using B, yfwd, P1, ybk; rep from * to last st; using A, K1.

PAVING border

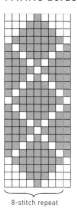

8-stitch repeat

KEY

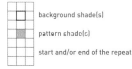

background shade(s)

pattern shade(s)

start and/or end of the repeat

NORWEGIAN STARS pattern (top section of picture)
STRIPED ribbing (middle section of picture)
PAVING border (bottom section of picture)

DOUBLE DIAMOND border

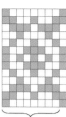

8-stitch repeat

REVERSE ZIGZAG peerie

6-stitch repeat

DAINTY OXO border

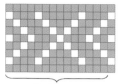

14-stitch repeat

FLOWERING TRELLIS border

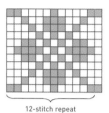

12-stitch repeat

CROWN peerie

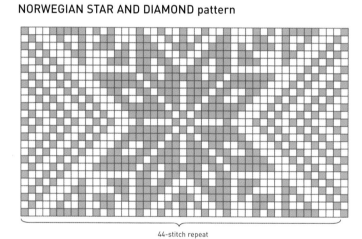

2-stitch repeat

NORWEGIAN STAR AND DIAMOND pattern

44-stitch repeat

KEY

☐ background shade(s)

☒ pattern shade(s)

☐ start and/or end of the repeat

Patterns in the picture, from the top: DOUBLE DIAMOND border,
CROWN peerie, FLOWERING TRELLIS border, REVERSE ZIGZAG peerie,
NORWEGIAN STAR AND DIAMOND pattern, REVERSE ZIGZAG peerie,
FLOWERING TRELLIS border, DAINTY OXO border

CHECKERBOARD pattern

Multiples of 4 sts plus 2

Row 1: (RS) Using A, K2; *using B, K2; using A, K2; rep from * to end.

Row 2: Using A, P2; *using B, P2; using A, P2; rep from * to end.

Row 3: Using B, K2; *using A, K2; using B, K2; rep from * to end.

Row 4: Using B, P2; *using A, P2; using B, P2; rep from * to end.

Rep these 4 rows.

HOUNDSTOOTH pattern

Multiples of 4 sts

Row 1: (RS) Using A, K2; *using B, K1; using A, K3; rep from * to last 2 sts; using B, K1; using A, K1.

Row 2: *Using A, P1; using B, P3; rep from * to end.

Row 3: *Using A, K1; using B, K3; rep from * to end.

Row 4: Using A, P2; *using B, P1; using A, P3; rep from * to last 2 sts; using B, P1; using A, P1.

Rep these 4 rows.

4-stitch repeat

DIAMOND jacquard

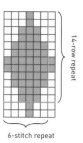

14-row repeat

6-stitch repeat

KEY

background shade(s)

pattern shade(s)

start and/or end of the repeat

CHECKERBOARD pattern (top section of picture)
HOUNDSTOOTH pattern (middle section of picture)
DIAMOND jacquard (bottom section of picture)

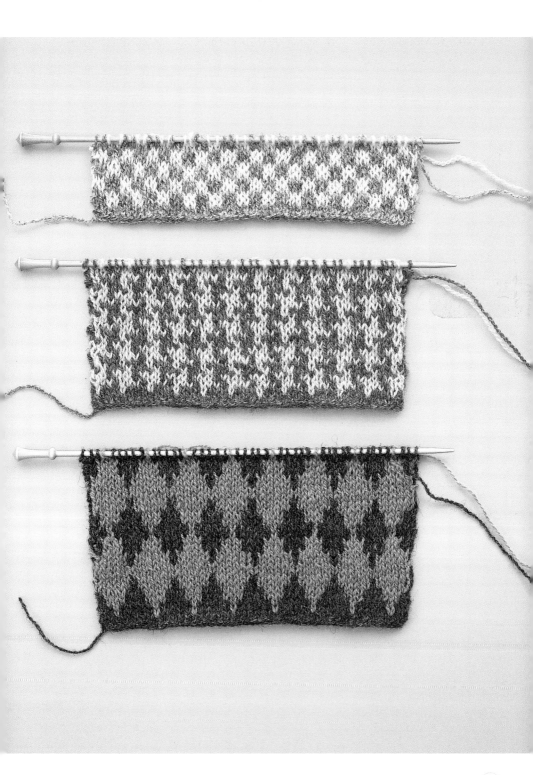

ARGYLE border

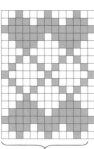

12-stitch repeat

SINGLE TRACK peerie

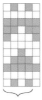

4-stitch repeat

BORDERED CHAIN pattern

4-stitch repeat

OXO pattern

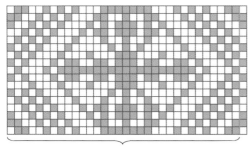

32-stitch repeat

HEARTS AND CROSS pattern

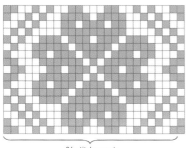

24-stitch repeat

KEY

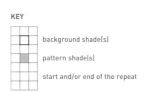

background shade(s)

pattern shade(s)

start and/or end of the repeat

Patterns in the picture, from the top: ARGYLE border,
BORDERED CHAIN pattern, OXO pattern,
SINGLE TRACK peerie, HEARTS AND CROSS pattern

ABSTRACT diamonds

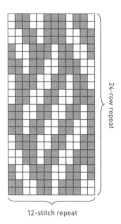

24-row repeat

12-stitch repeat

DOMINO pattern

8-stitch repeat

SAWTOOTH pattern

4-stitch repeat

KEY

background shade(s)

pattern shade(s)

start and/or end of the repeat

ABSTRACT diamonds (top section of picture)
DOMINO pattern (middle section of picture)
SAWTOOTH pattern (bottom section of picture)

236 Fair Isle

SIMPLE peerie

2-stitch repeat

CROSS peerie

4-stitch repeat

DIAMOND border

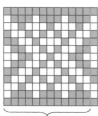

12-stitch repeat

STAR AND FIR TREE pattern

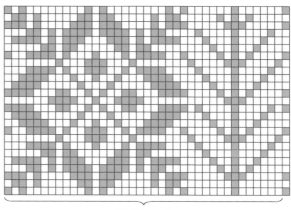

38-stitch repeat

DIAMOND AND BAR border

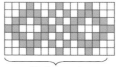

12-stitch repeat

SINGLE ZIGZAG peerie

4-stitch repeat

KEY

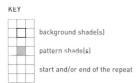

background shade(s)

pattern shade(s)

start and/or end of the repeat

Patterns in the picture, from the top: SIMPLE peerie,
CROSS peerie, DIAMOND AND BAR border,
STAR AND FIR TREE pattern, SINGLE ZIGZAG peerie,
DIAMOND border

OXO border

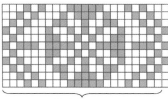

22-stitch repeat

BELT peerie

4-stitch repeat

OCTAGON AND BAR pattern

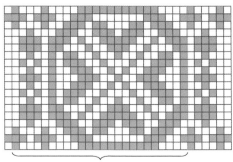

24-stitch repeat

FLOWER AND CROSS pattern

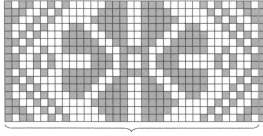

35-stitch repeat

WAVE peerie

12-stitch repeat

DIAMOND TRACK border

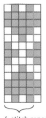

4-stitch repeat

KEY

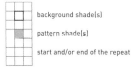

background shade(s)

pattern shade(s)

start and/or end of the repeat

Patterns in the picture, from the top: OXO border,
BELT peerie, FLOWER AND CROSS pattern, WAVE peerie,
OCTAGON AND BAR pattern, DIAMOND TRACK border

FLOWER AND CROSS checkerboard

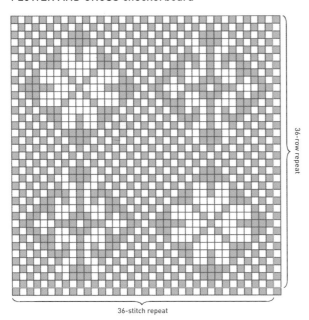

36-row repeat

36-stitch repeat

DIVIDED DIAMOND border

6-stitch repeat

GARTER peerie

5-stitch repeat

CHECKERBOARD peerie

4-stitch repeat

KEY

background shade(s)

pattern shade(s)

start and/or end of the repeat

Patterns in the picture, from the top: CHECKERBOARD peerie,
GARTER peerie, DIVIDED DIAMOND border,
FLOWER AND CROSS checkerboard

TRAVELING LEAF peerie

4-stitch repeat

BUCKLE peerie

8-stitch repeat

HEARTS border

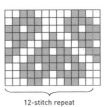

12-stitch repeat

SNOWFLAKE AND STAR border

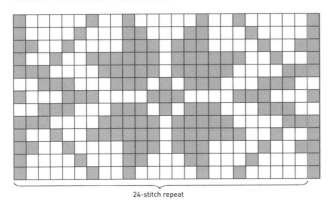

24-stitch repeat

KEY

▢	background shade(s)
▨	pattern shade(s)
	start and/or end of the repeat

HEARTS AND CHAIN pattern

38-stitch repeat

Patterns in the picture, from the top: HEARTS border,
SNOWFLAKE AND STAR border, BUCKLE peerie,
HEARTS AND CHAIN pattern, TRAVELING LEAF peerie

FLOWER checkerboard

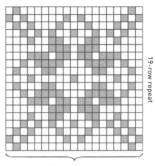

19-row repeat

19-stitch repeat

FLOWER AND CROSS peerie

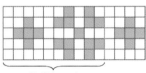

10-stitch repeat

FANCY ZIGZAG pattern

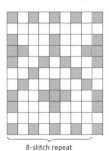

8-stitch repeat

Patterns in the picture, from the top: FLOWER checkerboard,
FLOWER AND CROSS peerie, FANCY ZIGZAG pattern,
FLOWER AND CROSS peerie

Glossary & index

Glossary

(Knitting tools are explained on page 10 and abbreviations on page 17.)

alpaca
yarn from alpacas and llamas

angora
yarn from Angora rabbits

Aran knitting
a type of traditional textured knitting originally from the isles of Aran, west of Ireland

bind off
to decrease stitches and bind off the last row of knitting

blocking
pinning down damp knitting so that it will dry to the correct shape and measurements

bobble
ball-shaped ornamental stitch on knit fabric

brocade
a knit fabric with a raised pattern

cable
a pattern of stitches that twist over and under each other to look like a rope or braid

cashmere
yarn from cashmere goats

cast on
to create new stitches as the foundation for knitting

checkerboard
a check pattern formed by alternating blocks of colored or patterned stitches

cotton
yarn from the cotton plant

crossed stitches
two sets of knit stitches crossing each other, with a purl stitch between the sets when there are more than two stitches

dye lot
the batch a yarn was dyed in; one dye lot can vary from another dye lot of the same shade

eyelet
a small decorative hole

fagotting
a stitch pattern of crossed threads formed into groups making an hourglass shape

Fair Isle knitting
a type of traditional colored knitting originally from Fair Isle in Shetland, north of Scotland; now used generically for Stockinette stitch patterns in which two colors are used alternately

and stranded across the back of the knitting when not in use

frill
wavy or pleated decorative edging

gansey
a type of traditional pullover sweater typically knitted in seafaring communities along the coasts of the British Isles

gauge swatch
a sample of knitting for counting the number of stitches and rows to a given measurement

grafting
binding off two edges together to form an invisible seam

in the round
circular knitting; knitting the front and back together as a tube so there are no side seams

insertion
a decorative strip that can be inserted into a piece of plain knit fabric

intarsia
multicolored knitting worked with separate balls of different colored yarns that are not carried across the back of the work

jacquard
a pattern knit directly into the fabric of a garment

kid mohair
yarn from Angora goat kids

knit stitch
a stitch that forms a flat vertical loop on the right side of the knitting

lamb's wool
yarn from the first shearing of a lamb

linen
yarn from the flax plant

merino wool
yarn from the fleece of merino sheep

mesh
a fabric characterized by its open appearance and the spaces between the yarn

mohair
yarn from Angora goats

motif
a decorative pattern that can be knit into a piece of plain knit fabric

net
an open fabric, created by connecting the intersections in a knitted construction to form a meshlike fabric

openwork
a knit fabric where yarns are twisted around each other to form lacy patterns

panel
piece of decorative knit fabric that is inserted into a piece of plain knit fabric

peerie
a narrow band of Fair Isle pattern comprising one to seven rows

ply
a single spun thread

purl stitch
a stitch that forms a horizontal loop on the right side of the knitting

reversible
stitch patterns that look identical on both sides or have one side that is the opposite of the other. Since there is no wrong side, they are used for projects where both sides of the work are visible, such as scarves

rib
vertical columns of knit and purl stitches, used at the edges of a garment for its elasticity

selvage
a neat and firm side edge

silk
yarn from silkworm cocoons

slip knot
a knot that can be loosened or tightened around the needle

slipping a stitch
transferring a stitch from one needle to the other without working a new stitch into it

smocking
a tightly gathered section of fabric, decoratively stitched

stranding
carrying one or two colors for short distances across the back of knitting until they are used again in a particular row

twisted stitches
one or more knit stitches traveling across a purl background

weaving
twisting yarns of different colors to incorporate them into the knitting ready to be used again in a specific row

weight
the thickness of a yarn

yarn over
the method of wrapping yarn around the needle to form a new stitch; there are different ways of wrapping the yarn depending on the stitch before and after the yarn over

Index

A

Abbreviations, 17
Abstract diamonds, 236
Acrylic yarn, 12
Alpaca yarn, 12
Alternating cable rib, 88
Alternating feather stitch, 188
Anchor motif, 66
Andalusian stitch, 56
Angora yarn, 12
Antler cable, 182
Apple leaves lace, 194
Aran designs, 90, 130, 162
Argyle border, 234
Asymmetric cable, 168

B

Back stitch, 39
Bamboo stitch, 102
Basic seed stitch, 46
Basic seed stitch panel, 62
Basket stitch, 54
Bead lace, 200
Beaded edging, 120
Beads, knitting in, 29
Bell motif, 132
Belt peerie, 240
Berry edging, 124
Binding off, 21
Bind-off fringe, 140
Bird's eye stitch, 218
Blackberry stitch, 94
Blanket rib, 86
Blocking, 36–37
Bluebell eyelets, 154
Bobbin, 10
Bobble brocade, 136
Bobble scallops pattern, 138
Bobble stitch, 130
Bordered chain pattern, 234
Bouclé yarn, 14
Braid cable, 182

Brick stitch, 214
British or Irish Moss stitch, 46
British or Irish moss stitch panel, 62
Broderie Anglais lace, 198
Broken chevron panel, 72
Buckle peerie, 244
Butterfly eyelets, 150
Buttonholes, 38

C

Cable and eyelet rib, 78
Cable and fan pattern, 172
Cable cast-on method, 20
Cable edging, 128
Cable needle, 10
Cabling, 28
Candlelight lace, 190
Care instruction symbols, 41
Caring for knitwear, 40, 41
Carrying yarn up the side, 30
Cashmere yarn, 12
Casting on, 19–20, 25
Cat's eye net, 190
Cat's paw eyelets, 158
Cell stitch, 194
Celtic cable, 166
Chain pattern, 224
Chain stitch loops, 140
Charts, using, 15–16
Checkerboard pattern, 232
Checkerboard peerie, 242
Chevron lace, 208
Chevron seed stitch, 48
Chevron stripes, 212
Circular needle, 10
Clam stitch, 100
Cloverleaf eyelets, 156
Cluster stitch, 108
Color, blocks of, working with, 32
Corded rib, 80
Cotton yarn, 12
Cross peerie, 238

Cross stitch, 104
Crossed cable pattern, 170
Crossed color stitch, 218
Crossed rib, 82
Crossed ribs with faggoting, 160
Crossed stitch, 210
Crossing stitches, 27
Crown of glory lace, 202
Crown peerie, 230

D

Dainty oxo border, 230
Daisy stitch, 132
Decreasing stitches, 26
Deep chevron pattern, 48
Diagonal grain stitch, 106
Diagonal rib, 78
Diagonal seed stitch, 50
Diamond and bar border, 238
Diamond border, 238
Diamond brocade, 46
Diamond edging, 122
Diamond eyelet boxes, 146
Diamond eyelet insertion, 160
Diamond eyelet pattern, 194
Diamond eyelets, 150
Diamond jacquard, 232
Diamond lace, 204
Diamond lace edging, 126
Diamond seed brocade, 52
Diamond seed stitch, 60
Diamond track border, 240
Diamond trellis pattern, 106
Divided diamond border, 242
Domino pattern, 236
Double cable, 166
Double diamond border, 230
Double diamond panel, 64
Double frill, 118
Double garter stitch edge, 33
Double herringbone panel, 74

Double honeycomb cable, 168
Double moss stitch, 48
Double-pointed needles, 10
Double rickrack rib, 88
Double trellis pattern, 104

E
Edgings, 110
Elongated stitch, 108
Elongating a stitch, 28
Embossed leaf motif, 132
Eyelet mock cable, 160
Eyelet rows, 146
Eyelet squares, 148
Eyelet stitch, 206
Eyelet triangles, 158

F
Fair Isle, 228
Falling leaves lace, 192
Fan edging, 124
Fan lace, 196
Fancy zigzag pattern, 246
Feather and fan lace, 202
Feather edging, 120
Feather rib, 88
Fern edging, 120
Fir cone lace, 208
Five-rib braid, 178
Flags and stripes panel, 72
Flower and cross checkerboard, 242
Flower and cross pattern, 240
Flower and cross peerie, 246
Flower checkerboard, 246
Flowering trellis border, 230
Flying eyelets, 150
Four-rib braid, 178
Four-stitch cable, 162
Four-stitch check, 52
Fuchsia pattern, 214

G
Gansey, 62
Garland stitch, 216
Garter eyelet diamonds, 148
Garter peerie, 242
Garter stitch, 44
Garter stitch frill, 114
Gathered stitch, 98
Gauge, 16
Gauge swatch, 16
Godmother's edging, 126
Gooseberry stitch, 90
Gothic lace, 198
Grapes panel, 142

H
Harris tweed stitch, 60
Hazelnut stitch, 130
Heart and star motifs, 68
Hearts and chain pattern, 244
Hearts and cross pattern, 234
Hearts border, 244
Holding yarn and needles, 18
Hollow oak with bobbles, 136
Honeycomb cable pattern, 172
Horizontal dash stitch, 54
Horseshoe lace, 202
Houndstooth pattern, 232

I
Increasing a stitch, 24–25
Increasing multiple stitches, 25
Instructions, using, 15
Interlocking leaves pattern, 106
Invisible cast-on method, 20

K
Kid mohair yarn, 12
Knit-on cast-on method, 20

Knit one, purl one rib, 76
Knit two, purl two rib, 76
Knitting needles, 10
Knitting stitches together, 26
Knotted edging, 116
Knotted mock cable, 134

L
Lace mesh, 208
Lacy edging, 122
Lacy rib, 84
Ladder eyelets, 154
Ladder panel, 66
Ladder stitch, 210
Lamb's lettuce lace, 190
Lamb's wool, 12
Lattice insertion, 152
Lattice pattern, 224
Lattice stitch, 184
Laundering, 40–41
Leaf edging, 128
Left-handed knitting, 22
Left-handed purling, 23
Lightning panel, 68
Linen stitch, 92
Linen yarn, 12
Link cable, 170
Little arrow stitch, 52
Lobster claw stitch, 166
Long bobble stitch, 90
Long loop edging, 116
Loop and braid edging, 126
Loop stitch, 140

M
Making a stitch, 24
Marriage lines panel, 68
Mattress stitch, 38
Medallion and antler cable, 176
Medallion panel, 170
Mercerized cotton yarn, 12
Merino wool, 12
Mistakes, correcting, 34–35
Mock cable rib, 82

Mock cables, 64
Mosaic stitch, 58
Moss diamond cable, 168
Moss stitch, 50
Moss tweed stitch, 210
Moss zigzag panel, 74

N
Needles and sizes, 10
Net pattern, 224
Norwegian star and
    diamond pattern, 230
Norwegian star pattern,
    228
Nosegay panel, 142

O
Octagon and bar pattern,
    240
Ogee lace, 204
Open diamond panel, 70
Open lattice stitch, 184
Open rope cable, 178
Open twisted rib, 82
Openwork edging, 122
Openwork rib, 86
Oriel lace, 200
Overlapping leaves pattern,
    102
Oxo border, 240
Oxo cable, 182
Oxo pattern, 234

P
Patchwork cable, 176
Paving border, 228
Peapod eyelets, 154
Pebble stitch, 96
Pennant stitch, 56
Picking up dropped stitches,
    34, 35
Picking up new stitches, 37
Picot ridge hem, 110
Pilling, removing, 40
Pinecone eyelets, 156
Plain bind off, 21

Plaited basket stitch, 96
Ply, 12
Polyester yarn, 12
Popcorn stitch, 130
Pressing, 37
Print o' the wave lace, 206
Purl ridge hem, 110
Purling, 23
Purling stitches together, 26
Pyramid stitch, 58

Q
Quatrefoil eyelets, 148

R
Raised eyelet rib, 86
Random-dyed yarn, 14
Repairs, minor, 41
Reverse stockinette stitch,
    44
Reverse zigzag peerie, 230
Rib checkerboard, 50
Ribbed cable, 176
Ribbon stitch, 226
Ribs, 76
Rickrack rib, 80
Ridge and furrow panel, 64
Ridged check stitch, 220
Ridged slip stitch, 98
Ridged stripes, 218
Right-handed knitting, 22
Right-handed purling, 23
Ripple stitch, 104
Risotto stitch, 100
Rosary stitch, 156
Rough marriage lines panel,
    70
Row counter, 10
Ruffled edging, 116

S
Sand pattern, 162
Satin loop edging, 114
Sawtooth pattern, 236
Scallop edging, 118
Scallop insertion, 152

Seam bind off, 21
Securing yarn end, 21
Seeded cable, 180
Seeded check, 58
Seeded flags panel, 70
Seeded rib, 76
Selvages, 33
Sequins, knitting in, 29
Serrated edging, 128
Sewing up, 38–39
Silk yarn, 12
Simple lace, 188
Simple lace edging, 114
Simple loop edging, 112
Simple peerie, 238
Simple seed texture stitch,
    46
Simple star motif, 72
Single cast-on method, 20
Single frill, 118
Single garter stitch edge, 33
Single seed stitch edge, 33
Single stockinette stitch
    edge, 33
Single track peerie, 234
Single zigzag peerie, 238
Six-stitch cable, 164
Six-stitch cable variation,
    164
Slip knot, 19
Slip marker, 10
Slip stitch decrease, 26
Slip stitch lace, 196
Slip stitch rows, 216
Slip stitch stripes, 222
Slipped granite stitch, 92
Smocked honeycomb, 136
Smocking, 142
Snags, repairing, 40
Snowdrop eyelets, 144
Snowdrop lace, 200
Snowflake and star border,
    244
Snowflake eyelets, 144
Space-dyed yarn, 14
Spanish lace, 186

Spine stitch, 94
Spiral rib, 78
Spray edging, 124
St. John's Wort stitch, 198
Star and fir tree pattern, 238
Steps panel, 66
Stitch holder, 10
Stitch marker, 10
Stockinette stitch, 44
Stockinette stitch check, 54
Stockinette stitch edging, 110
Stockinette stitch flags panel, 74
Storing knitted items, 40
Stranded cable, 180
Stranding, 30–31
Striped ribbing, 228
Supple rib, 84
Swatch, 16
Sycamore eyelets, 146

T
Tapestry stitch, 212
Three-color linen stitch, 214
Three-color oak stitch, 226
Three-color tweed stitch, 220
Thumb cast-on method, 19
Tied cable, 174
Trailing leaves pattern, 192
Traveling fern pattern, 188
Traveling leaf peerie, 244
Traveling vine lace, 206
Tree of life edging, 112
Tree of life panel, 62
Trellis cable, 164
Trellis pattern, 90
Trellis stitch, 96
Trinity stitch, 92
Tucked stockinette stitch, 98
Turkish stitch, 192
Twin leaf pattern, 196
Twisted cable, 180
Twisted Celtic cable, 184

Twisted path cable, 174
Twisted rib, 80
Twisting stitches, 27
Two-color granite stitch, 222
Two-color hurdle stitch, 222
Two-color loop stitch, 210
Two-color oak stitch, 226
Two-color rice stitch, 212
Two-color star stitch, 216
Two-color tweed stitch, 220

U
Unraveling, 34, 35

V
Vandyke eyelet rows, 144
Vandyke eyelets, 158
Vertical caterpillar stitch, 60
Vine lace, 204
Viscose yarn, 12

W
Waffle stitch, 100
Washing instructions and symbols, 41
Wave edging, 112
Wave peerie, 240
Waved welt stitch, 56
Wavy cable, 172
Weaving, 31
Weaving in ends, 36
Weight, 12
Wheatear pattern, 138
Wild oats pattern, 174
Woven brocade, 94
Woven butterfly stitch, 108
Woven ladder stitch, 102
Woven rib, 84

Y
Yarn-over increases, 24–25

Z
Zigzag insertion, 152

Art Editor: Sarah Rock
Photography: Deirdre Rooney
Illustration: Stephen Pollitt
Knitters: Lisa Allan, Karen Hemingway,
Ruth Hereward-Isaac, Pauline Hornsby

Note: see www.cobweb.net/~knitting/lefties
for a reworking of abbreviations for left-
handed knitters.

Copyright © 2007 by Marabout, Paris

First published in the United States in 2007
by Watson-Guptill Publications,
a division of Nielsen Business Media, Inc.,
770 Broadway, New York, N.Y. 10003
www.watsonguptill.com

ISBN-10: 0-8230-9957-1
ISBN-13: 978-0-8230-9957-3

Library of Congress Control Number: 2007926725

Printed in Singapore at Tien Wah Press

First printing, 2007

1 2 3 4 5 / 11 10 09 08 07